LIB
UNIVERSITY LU.   W9-CHX-913
1020 S. HARRISON ROAD
EAST LANSING, MI 48823

GOSPEL:
THE LIFE OF JESUS
AS TOLD BY THE
WORLD'S GREATEST
WRITERS

Compiled by
Constance Pollock & Daniel Pollock

WORD PUBLISHING
Nashville • London • Vancouver • Melbourne

For our dear Edward

Word Publishing

Copyright © 1998 by Constance Pollock and Daniel Pollock

No portion of this book may be reproduced, stored in a retrieval system, or transmitted in any form or by any means—electronic, mechanical, photocopy, recording, or any other—except for brief quotations in printed reviews, without the prior written permission of the publisher.

All scripture quotations are taken from the King James Version of the Bible.

Book design by Kandi Shepherd

Library of Congress Cataloging-in-Publication Data

Pollock, Constance.
 Gospel : the life of Jesus as told by the world's great writers / by Constance and Dan Pollock.
  p. cm.
 Includes bibliographical references and index.
 ISBN 0-8499-1544-9
 1. Jesus Christ—Literary collections. I. Pollock, Daniel. 1944– . I. Title.
PN6071.J4P57 1998
808.8'0351—dc21   97-32772
                CIP

Printed in the United States of America
8 9 0 1 2 3 4 5 6 BVG 9 8 7 6 5 4 3 2 1

CONTENTS

Acknowledgments - - - - - - - - - - - - - - - - - - V

Introduction - IX

In the Beginning - - - - - - - - - - - - - - - - - - - 1

Announcements - - - - - - - - - - - - - - - - - - - 5

Birth - 17

The Ministry - 55

The Passion - 139

The Crucifixion - - - - - - - - - - - - - - - - - - 173

The Resurrection - - - - - - - - - - - - - - - - - 201

Biographical Notes - - - - - - - - - - - - - - - 213

Index of Authors - - - - - - - - - - - - - - - - - 241

ACKNOWLEDGMENTS

Grateful acknowledgment is made to the following authors and publishers who have given permission to use copyrighted material:

A. P. Watt Ltd. on behalf of The Royal Literary Fund for "The Donkey," "The Convert," and "Joseph" by G. K. Chesterton.

Liveright Publishing Corporation for "a man who had fallen among thieves," copyright © 1926, 1954, 1991 by the Trustees for the E. E. Cummings Trust. Copyright © 1985 by George James Firmage, from *Complete Poems: 1904-1962* by E. E. Cummings. Edited by George J. Firmage.

Faber and Faber Ltd. and Harcourt Brace & Company for "Journey of the Magi" in *Collected Poems 1909-1962* by T. S. Eliot. Copyright © 1936 by Harcourt Brace & Company, copyright 1964, 1963 by T. S. Eliot.

Harcourt Brace & Company for "A Song for Simeon" from Collected Poems 1909-1962 by T. S. Eliot. Copyright © 1936 by Harcourt Brace & Company, copyright 1964, 1963 by T. S. Eliot.

Henry Holt and Company, Inc., and Random House UK Limited for "Sycamore" from *The Poetry of Robert Frost*, edited by Edward Connery Lathem, Copyright 1942, © 1970 by Lesley Frost Ballantine, © 1969 by Henry Holt and Company, Inc. and Jonathan Cape.

Carcanet Press Limited and Oxford University Press, Inc., for "The Fallen Tower of Siloam" in *Collected Poems 1975* by Robert Graves. Copyright © 1988 by Robert Graves.

Henry Holt and Company, Inc., and the Society of Authors as the Literary Representative of the Estate of A. E. Housman, for excerpt "XLV" from "A Shropshire Lad" by A. E. Housman, from *The Collected Poems of A. E. Housman* by A. E. Housman, Copyright 1939, 1940 by Henry Holt and Company, Inc., © 1967 by Robert E. Symons.

Viking Penguin, a division of Penguin Books USA, Inc., and Laurence Pollinger Limited and the Estate of Frieda Lawrence Ravagli for "Tortoise Shell" by D.H. Lawrence from *The Complete Poems of D.H. Lawrence* by D. H. Lawrence, edited by V. de Sola Pinto & F. W. Roberts. Copyright © 1964, 1971 by Angelo Ravagli and C. M. Weekley, Executors of the Estate of Frieda Lawrence Ravagli.

Harcourt Brace & Company for "The Holy

Innocents" from *Lord Weary's Castle*, copyright 1946 and renewed 1974 by Robert Lowell.

New Directions Publishing Corporation for "Cana" by Thomas Merton from *The Collected Poems of Thomas Merton*. Copyright © 1946 by New Directions Publishing Corporation, 1977 by The Trustees of the Merton Legacy Trust.

Elizabeth Barnett, literary executor, for "Jesus to His Disciples" by Edna St. Vincent Millay. From Collected Poems, HarperCollins. Copyright © 1954, 1982 by Norma Millay Ellis. All rights reserved.

W. W. Norton & Company, Inc., for "Joseph's Suspicion," "The Last Supper," and "The Garden of Olives" from *Translations From the Poetry of Rainer Maria Rilke* by Rainer Maria Rilke, translated by M. D. Herter Norton. Translation copyright 1938 by W. W. Norton & Company, Inc., renewed © 1966 by M. D. Herter Norton.

David Curzon and Will Alexander Washburn, translators, for "Mary's Visitation" by Rainer Maria Rilke.

Harcourt Brace & Company for "Special Starlight" from *The Complete Poems of Carl Sandburg*, copyright 1950 by Carl Sandburg and renewed 1978 by Margaret Sandburg, Helga Sandburg, Crile, and Janet Sandburg.

The Estate of Dorothy Sayers and the Watkins/Loomis Agency for two extracts from *The Man Born To Be King*, written for broadcasting by

Dorothy L. Sayers. Published by Harper & Brothers. Copyright 1943 by Dorothy L. Sayers.

Sinclair Stevenson for the extract from "Still Falls the Rain" from *Collected Poems of Edith Sitwell*.

New Directions Publishing Corporation and J. M. Dent & Sons for extracts from "In the Beginning" by Dylan Thomas, from *The Poems of Dylan Thomas*. Copyright © 1953 by Dylan Thomas, and "This Bread I Break" by Dylan Thomas, from *The Poems of Dylan Thomas*. Copyright © 1967 by The Trustees for the Copyrights of Dylan Thomas.

Every effort has been made by the editors to contact the owners of the copyrighted material in this book. If we have inadvertently failed to acknowledge anyone, we will include appropriate notice in any future edition.

INTRODUCTION

In 1870, on the day before he died, Charles Dickens wrote in a letter: "I have always striven in my writings to express veneration for the life and lessons of Our Saviour, because I feel it." With this simple, heartfelt testimony, Dickens could well have been speaking for many beloved writers over the centuries, for whom the Gospel has been a primary inspiration.

You will find artful evidence of their testimony in this collection of poetry, prose, and drama. The diverse voices of Emily Dickinson and Lewis Carroll, Elizabeth Barrett Browning and Henry Wadsworth Longfellow, Edna St. Vincent Millay and Thomas Hardy were all inspired by the Gospel narrative and have been arranged in harmony with Matthew, Mark, Luke, and John. Each selection has a corresponding scriptural reference.

Two revered novelists—Dickens and Leo Tolstoy—recounted the "greatest story ever told," putting the Gospels into simplified, didactic form. Dickens did this for his sons and daughters; Tolstoy wanted to instruct the children of his village. "The teaching of Christ," Tolstoy explained, "shows men that good comes to them by love and that all can have this good. That is why the teaching of Christ is called the Evangel. *Ev* means 'good,' *angelion* means 'tidings'—good tidings."

Over the years, it seems no incident or parable from the "good tidings" has escaped the attention of these literary lights. We offer here those we found especially meaningful, moving, and sometimes surprising. An excerpt from *Jane Eyre* shows Charlotte Brontë to be intimately acquainted with the Bible. The brilliant, troubled Welsh poet Dylan Thomas celebrated the Word in the beginning and the Word made flesh. In a harrowing poem about the World War II blitz, British poetess Edith Sitwell compared the bombs falling on London to the hammer blows nailing Jesus to the cross. Of course, the most dramatic events in the Gospel narrative—the Annunciation, the Birth, the Passion, the Crucifixion, the Resurrection—have several entries each, since they overwhelmingly impressed the creative imaginations.

But there's more than just fanciful poetic or reverent retellings. For example, Thornton Wilder, author of that American stage perennial, *Our Town*, has here a playlet about the *Flight Into*

Egypt. Mary and Joseph, to be sure, are main characters; but so is the transportation—Hepzibah, the donkey. She grumbles to Our Lady about the hurry and propounds an important theological question: Why is this Baby to be spared in Herod's slaughter of the Holy Innocents? Another beast of burden touched by glory and hosannas is given voice in G. K. Chesterton's poem, "The Donkey."

Edmond Rostand, the famous French playwright of the enduring *Cyrano de Bergerac*, was inspired by the story of the woman of Samaria at the well to write a three-act drama, *La Samaritaine*, performed originally by Sarah Bernhardt. In it the saucy Photine spars verbally with the Stranger who tastes her water before she gradually realizes it is He who offers her the greater gift, the Living Water.

Another writer—Dorothy Sayers, far better known for her popular detective novels, the Lord Peter Wimsey series—provides a vivid setting to several of Christ's miracles. Scripted originally as radio dramas, they are excerpted here to be read and savored.

In all cases the writers have clearly cherished the biblical text before taking their resourceful leaps into poetry, prose, and dramatic dialogue. Two examples of this are the delicate and reclusive poetesses, Emily Dickinson and Christina Rossetti, both of whom often used the Bible as a sourcebook for their verse. Rossetti's brother William said his sister's writing offered "the ardent absorbing devotion to the work and the very person of the Saviour

Jesus Christ." And Dickinson's sister Lavinia found among Emily's personal belongings after her death a scrap of paper with three words that pinpoint the wellspring of her genius: "Grasped by God."

But the "good tidings" find resonance here in full literary chorus—from the erudite John Milton and Alexander Pope to the plain-speaking Robert Frost and Carl Sandburg; from the Slavic souls of Ivan Turgenev and Boris Pasternak to the Teutonic voices of J. W. von Goethe and Ranier Maria Rilke; from the syncopated rhythms of Gerard Manley Hopkins and E. E. Cummings to the traditional meters of Nathaniel Hawthorne and Rudyard Kipling.

Because this is not a scholarly work, for clarity and brevity we have sometimes modernized language and regretfully shortened passages. We hope readers will be intrigued by these selections and search out complete texts and other offerings from these authors, whose capsule biographies follow the text. It is also our hope that this book will be a revelation in its own earthly way—illumination to students of the Bible and to lovers of literature as well.

—CONSTANCE AND DANIEL POLLOCK

IN THE BEGINNING

*I*am very anxious that you should know something about the History of Jesus Christ. For everybody ought to know about Him. No one ever lived who was so good, so kind, so gentle, and so sorry for all people who did wrong, or were in any way ill or miserable, as He was. And as He is now in Heaven, where we hope to go, and all to meet each other after we are dead, and there be happy always together. You never can think what a good place Heaven is, without knowing who He was and what He did.

—CHARLES DICKENS (TO HIS CHILDREN)

In the beginning was the Word, and the Word was with God, and the Word was God. The same was

in the beginning with God. All things were made by Him; and without Him was not any thing made that was made. In Him was life; and the life was the light of men. And the light shineth in darkness; and the darkness comprehended it not.

John 1:1—5

In the Beginning

In the beginning was the three-pointed star,
One smile of light across the empty face;
One bough of bone across the rooting air,
The substance forked that marrowed the first sun;
And, burning ciphers on the round of space,
Heaven and hell mixed as they spun.

In the beginning was the pale signature,
Three-syllabled and starry as the smile;
And after came the imprints on the water,
Stamp of the minted face upon the moon;
The blood that touched the crosstree and the grail
Touched the first cloud and left a sign.

In the beginning was the mounted fire
That set alight the weathers from a spark,
A three-eyed, red-eyed spark, blunt as a flower;
Life rose and spouted from the rolling seas,
Burst in the roots, pumped from the earth and rock

In the Beginning

The secret oils that drive the grass.

In the beginning was the word, the word
That from the solid bases of the light
Abstracted all the letters of the void;
And from the cloudy bases of the breath
The word flowed up, translating to the heart
First characters of birth and death.

—Dylan Thomas

Announcements

And in the sixth month the angel Gabriel was sent from God unto a city of Galilee, named Nazareth, to a virgin espoused to a man whose name was Joseph, of the house of David; and the virgin's name was Mary.

LUKE 1:26—27

Angel-Watered Lily

This is that blessed Mary, pre-elect
God's Virgin. Gone is a great while, and she
Dwelt young in Nazareth of Galilee.
Unto God's will she brought devout respect,
Profound simplicity of intellect
And supreme patience. From her mother's knee

Faithful and hopeful; wise in charity;
Strong in grave peace; in pity circumspect.
So held she through her girlhood; as it were
An angel-watered lily, that near God
Grown and is quiet. Till, one dawn at home
She woke in her white bed and had no fear
At all, yet wept till sunshine, and felt awed
Because the fullness of the time was come.

—DANTE GABRIEL ROSSETTI

*And the angel came in unto her, and said, Hail, thou
that art highly favoured, the Lord is with thee:
blessed art thou among women.*

LUKE 1:28

Mary and Gabriel

Young Mary, loitering once her garden way,
Felt a warm splendour grow in the April day,
As wine that blushes water through. And soon,
Out of the gold air of the afternoon,
One knelt before her: hair he had, or fire,
Bound back above his ears with golden wire,
Baring the eager marble of his face.
Not man's or woman's was the immortal grace

Rounding the limbs beneath that robe of white,
And lighting the proud eyes with changeless light,
Incurious. Calm as his wings, and fair,
That presence filled the garden.

    She stood there,
Saying, "What would you, Sir?"

    He told his word,
"Blessed art thou of women!" Half she heard,
Hands folded and face bowed, half long had known,
The message of that clear and holy tone,
That fluttered hot sweet sobs about her heart;
Such serene tidings moved such human smart.
Her breath came quick as little flakes of snow.
Her hands crept up her breast. She did but know
It was not hers. She felt a trembling stir
Within her body, a will too strong for her
That held and filled and mastered all. With eyes
Closed, and a thousand soft short broken sighs,
She gave submission; fearful, meek, and glad . . .

She wished to speak. Under her breasts she had
Such multitudinous burnings, to and fro,
And throbs not understood; she did not know
If they were hurt or joy for her; but only
That she was grown strange to herself, half lonely,
All wonderful, filled full of pains to come
And thoughts she dare not think, swift thoughts
    and dumb,
Human, and quaint, her own, yet very far,
Divine, dear, terrible, familiar . . .
Her heart was faint for telling; to relate

Her limbs' sweet treachery, her strange high estate,
Over and over, whispering, half revealing,
Weeping; and so find kindness to her healing.
'Twixt tears and laughter, panic hurrying her,
She raised her eyes to that fair messenger.
He knelt unmoved, immortal; with his eyes
Gazing beyond her, calm to the calm skies;
Radiant, untroubled in his wisdom, kind.
His sheaf of lilies stirred not in the wind.
How should she, pitiful with mortality,
Try the wide peace of that felicity
With ripples of her perplexed shaken heart,
And hints of human ecstasy, human smart,
And whispers of the lonely weight she bore,
And how her womb within was hers no more
And at length hers?
         Being tired, she bowed her head;
And said, "So be it!"
         The great wings were spread
Showering glory on the fields, and fire.
The whole air, singing, bore him up, and higher,
Unswerving, unreluctant. Soon he shone
A gold speck in the gold skies; then was gone.

The air was colder, and grey. She stood alone.

—RUPERT BROOKE

*And the angel said unto her, Fear not, Mary: for
thou hast found favour with God. And, behold,*

8

thou shalt conceive in thy womb, and bring forth a son, and shalt call his name JESUS. He shall be great, and shall be called the Son of the Highest: and the Lord God shall give unto him the throne of his father David: And he shall reign over the house of Jacob for ever; and of his kingdom there shall be no end.

LUKE 1:30—33

A Virgin Shall Conceive, a Virgin Bear a Son!

A Virgin shall conceive, a Virgin bear a Son!
From Jesse's root behold a Branch arise,
Whose sacred Flow'r with Fragrance fills the Skies.
Th'Aethereal Spirit o'er its Leaves shall move,
And on its Top descends the Mystic Dove.
Ye Heav'ns! from high the dewy Nectar pour,
And in soft Silence shed the kindly Show'r!
The Sick and Weak the healing Plant shall aid;
From Storms a Shelter, and from Head a Shade.
All Crimes shall cease, and ancient Fraud shall fail;
Returning Justice lift aloft her Scale;
Peace o'er the World her Olive-Wand extend,
And white-rob'd Innocence from Heav'n descend.
Swift fly the Years, and rise th'expected Morn!
Oh spring to Light, Auspicious Babe, be born!

—ALEXANDER POPE

Now the birth of Jesus Christ was on this wise:
When as His mother Mary was espoused to Joseph,
before they came together, she was found with child
of the Holy Ghost. Then Joseph her husband, being
a just man, and not willing to make her a public
example, was minded to put her away privily. But
while he thought on these things, behold, the angel
of the Lord appeared unto him in a dream, saying,
Joseph, thou son of David, fear not to take unto
thee Mary thy wife: for that which is conceived in
her is of the Holy Ghost. And she shall bring forth
a son, and thou shalt call His name JESUS: for He
shall save His people from their sins. Now all this
was done, that it might be fulfilled which was spo-
ken of the Lord by the prophet, saying, Behold, a
virgin shall be with child, and shall bring forth a
son, and they shall call his name Emmanuel, which
being interpreted is, God with us.

MATTHEW 1:18—23

Joseph's Suspicion

And the angel spoke and made an effort
with the man, who clenched his fists;
But dost thou not see by every fold
that she is cool as God's early day?

Yet the other looked somberly at him,

murmuring only: What has changed her so?
But at that the angel cried: Carpenter,
dost thou not yet see that the Lord God is acting?

Because thou makest boards, in thy pride,
wouldst thou really call him to account
who modestly out of the same wood
makes leaves burgeon and buds swell?

He understood. And as he now raised his eyes
very frightened, to the angel,
he was gone. He pushed his heavy
cap slowly off, Then he sang praise.

—Rainer Maria Rilke

*Then Joseph being raised from sleep did as the
angel of the Lord had bidden him, and took unto
him his wife: And knew her not till she had brought
forth her firstborn son: and he called His name
JESUS.*

Matthew 1:24—25

Joseph

If the stars fell; night's nameless dreams
　　Of bliss and blasphemy came true, .
If skies were green and snow were gold,
　　And you loved me as I love you;

O long light hands and curled brown hair,
　　And eyes where sits a naked soul;
Dare I even then draw near and burn
　　My fingers in the aureole?

Yes, in the one wise foolish hour
　　God gives this strange strength to a man.
He can demand, though not deserve,
　　Where ask he cannot, seize he can.

But once the blood's wild wedding o'er,
　　Were not dread his, half dark desire,
To see the Christ-child in the cot,
　　The Virgin Mary by the fire?

　　　　　　　　　　　　—G. K. CHESTERTON

*And Mary said, My soul doth magnify the Lord,
And my spirit hath rejoiced in God my Saviour. For
He hath regarded the low estate of His handmaid-
en: for, behold, from henceforth all generations
shall call me blessed. For He that is mighty hath
done to me great things; and holy is His name. And*

His mercy is on them that fear Him from genera-
tion to generation. He hath shown strength with
His arm; He hath scattered the proud in the imagi-
nation of their hearts. He hath put down the
mighty from their seats, and exalted them of low
degree. He hath filled the hungry with good things;
and the rich He hath sent empty away. He hath
helped His servant Israel, in remembrance of His
mercy; As he spake to our fathers, to Abraham, and
to His seed for ever.

LUKE 1:46—55

The May Magnificat

May is Mary's month, and I
Muse at that and wonder why:
    Her feasts follow reason,
    Dated due to season—

Candlemas, Lady Day;
But the Lady Month, May,
    Why fasten that upon her,
    With a feasting in her honour?

Is it only its being brighter
Than the most are must delight her?
    Is it opportunest
    And flowers finds soonest?

Ask of her, the mighty mother:
Her reply puts this other
    Question: What is Spring?—
    Growth in everything—

Flesh and fleece, fur and feather,
Grass and greenworld all together;
    Star-eyed strawberry-breasted
    Throstle above her nested

Cluster of bugle blue eggs thin
Forms and warms the life within;
    And bird and blossom swell
    In sod or sheath or shell.

All things rising, all things sizing
Mary sees, sympathising
    With that world of good,
    Nature's motherhood.

Their magnifying of each its kind
With delight calls to mind
    How she did in her stored
    Magnify the Lord.

Well but there was more than this:
Spring's universal bliss
    Much, had much to say
    To offering Mary May.

When drop-of-blood-and-foam-dapple
Bloom lights the orchard-apple
    And thicket and thorp are merry
    With silver-surfed cherry

And azuring-over greybell makes
Wood banks and brakes wash wet like lakes
    and magic cuckoocall
    Caps, clears, and clinches all—

This ecstasy all through mothering earth
Tells Mary her mirth till Christ's birth
    To remember and exultation
    In God who was her salvation.

—GERARD MANLEY HOPKINS

And Mary arose in those days, and went into the hill country with haste, into a city of Judah; And entered into the house of Zacharias, and saluted Elisabeth. And it came to pass, that, when Elisabeth heard the salutation of Mary, the babe leaped in her womb; and Elisabeth was filled with the Holy Ghost: And she spake out with a loud voice, and said, Blessed art thou among women, and blessed is the fruit of thy womb. And whence is this to me, that the mother of my Lord should

come to me? For, lo, as soon as the voice of thy salutation sounded in mine ears, the babe leaped in my womb for joy.

LUKE 1:39—44

Mary's Visitation

At the outset she still carried it quite well
but already, from time to time, when climbing, she
became aware of the marvel of her belly,—
and then she stood, caught breath, up on the high

Judean hills. It was not the land
but her abundance that spread out around her;
going on she felt: you couldn't have more than
the largess that she now perceived.

And it urged her to lay her hand
on the other belly, which was heavier.
And the women swayed toward each other
and touched each other's garb and hair.

Each, filled with her sanctified possession,
had the protection of a woman friend.
In her, the Saviour still was a bud intact,
but the Baptist in the womb of her "aunt"
already leapt, seized with delight.

—RAINER MARIA RILKE

BIRTH

Some say that ever 'gainst that season comes
Wherein our Saviour's birth is celebrated,
The bird of dawning singeth all night long;
And then, they say, no spirit can walk abroad;
The nights are wholesome; then no planets strike,
No fairy takes, nor witch hath power to charm,
So hallow'd and so gracious is the time.

—William Shakespeare (from Hamlet)

And she brought forth her firstborn son, and wrapped Him in swaddling clothes, and laid Him in a manger; because there was no room for them in the inn.

Luke 2:7

Gates and Doors

There was a gentle hostler
(And blessed be his name!)
He opened up the stable
That night Our Lady came.
Our Lady and Saint Joseph,
He gave them food and bed,
And Jesus Christ has given him
A glory round his head.

So let the gate swing open
However poor the yard,
Lest weary people visit you
And find their passage barred;
Unlatch the door at midnight
And let your lantern's glow
Shine out to guide the traveller's feet
To you across the snow.

There was a courteous hostler
(He is in Heaven tonight!)
He held Our Lady's bridle
And helped her to alight;
He spread clean straw before her
Whereon she might lie down,
And Jesus Christ has given him
An everlasting crown.

Unlock the door this evening,
And let your gate swing wide,

BIRTH

Let all who ask for shelter
Come speedily inside,
What if your house be small?
There is a Guest is coming
Will glorify it all.

There was a joyous hostler
Who knelt on Christmas morn
Beside the radiant manger
Wherein his Lord was born.
His heart was full of laughter
His soul was full of bliss
When Jesus, on His Mother's lap
Gave him His hand to kiss.

Unbar your heart this evening
And keep no stranger out.
Take from your soul's great portal
The barrier of doubt.
To humble folk and weary
Give hearty welcoming,
Your breast shall be tomorrow
The cradle of a King.

—JOYCE KILMER

And it came to pass, as the angels were gone away from them into heaven, the shepherds said one to another, Let us now go even unto Bethlehem, and

see this thing which is come to pass, which the Lord hath made known unto us. And they came with haste, and found Mary, and Joseph, and the babe lying in a manger. And when they had seen it, they made known abroad the saying which was told them concerning this child.

Luke 2:15—17

The Shepherds

The shepherds went their hasty way,
    And found the lowly stable-shed,
Where the virgin-mother lay:
    And now they checked their eager tread,
For to the babe, that at her bosom clung,
A mother's song the virgin-mother sung.

They told her how a glorious light,
    Streaming from a heavenly throng,
Around them shone, suspending night,
    While, sweeter than a mother's song,
Blest angels heralded the Saviour's birth,
Glory to God on high! and peace on earth.

She listened to the tale divine,
    And closer still the babe she pressed;
And while she cried, "The babe is mine!"
    The milk rushed faster to her breast:

Joy rose within her, like a summer's morn;
Peace, peace on earth! the Prince of peace is born.

—Samuel Taylor Coleridge

Now when Jesus was born in Bethlehem of Judaea in the days of Herod the king, behold, there came wise men from the east to Jerusalem.

Matthew 2:1

Ode on the Morning of Christ's Nativity

This is the month, and this the happy morn,
Wherein the Son of heaven's eternal King,
Of wedded maid and virgin mother born,
Our great redemption from above did bring;
For so the holy sages once did sing,
    That he our deadly forfeit should release,
And with his Father work us a perpetual peace.

That glorious form, that light insufferable,
And that far-beaming blaze of majesty,
Where with he wont at heaven's high council-table
To sit the midst of trinal unity,
He laid aside; and here with us to be,
    Forsook the courts of everlasting day,

And chose with us a darksome house of mortal clay.

Say, heavenly muse, shall not thy sacred vein
Afford a present to the infant God?
Hast thou no verse, no hymn, or solemn strain,
To welcome him to this his new abode,
Now while the heaven, by the sun's team untrod,
 Hath took no print of the approaching light,
And all the spangled host keep watch in squadrons
 bright?

See how from far upon the eastern road
The star-led wizards haste with odours sweet!
O run, prevent them with thy humble ode,
And lay it lowly at his blessed feet;
Have thou the honour first thy Lord to greet,
 And join thy voice unto the angel quire,
From out his secret altar touched with hallowed fire.

         —JOHN MILTON

A Christmas Carol

In the bleak mid-winter
 Frosty wind made moan,
Earth stood hard as iron,
 Water like a stone;
Snow had fallen, snow on snow,
 Snow on snow,

In the bleak mid-winter
    Long ago.

Our God, heaven cannot hold him,
    Nor earth sustain;
Heaven and earth shall flee away
    When he comes to reign:
In the bleak mid-winter
    A stable-place sufficed
The Lord God Almighty
    Jesus Christ.

Enough for him whom cherubim
    Worship night and day,
A breastful of milk
    And a mangerful of hay;
Enough for him whom angels
    Fall down before,
The ox and ass and camel
    Which adore.

Angels and archangels
    May have gathered there,
Cherubim and seraphim
    Thronged the air,
But only his mother
    In her maiden bliss
Worshipped the Beloved
    With a kiss.

What can I give him,

Poor as I am?
If I were a shepherd
 I would bring a lamb,
If I were a wise man
 I would do my part—
Yet what I can I give him,
 Give my heart.

    —CHRISTINA GEORGINA ROSSETTI

A Hymn on the Nativity of My Savior

I sing the birth, was born tonight,
The Author both of life and light;
 The angels so did sound it,
And like the ravished shepherds said,
Who saw the light and were afraid,
 Yet searched, and true they found it.

The Son of God, the Eternal King,
That did us all salvation bring,
 And freed the soul from danger;
He whom the whole world could not take,
The Word, which heaven and earth did make,
 Was now laid in a manger.

The Father's wisdom willed it so,
The son's obedience knew no No,
 Both wills were in one stature;

And as that wisdom had decreed,
The Word was now made flesh indeed,
    And took on Him our nature.

What comfort by Him do we win?
Who made Himself the Prince of sin
    To make us heirs of glory?
To see this Babe, all innocence;
A Martyr born in our defense;
    Can man forget this story?

—Ben Jonson

Special Starlight

The Creator of night and of birth
was the Maker of the stars.
Shall we look up now at stars in Winter
And call them always sweeter friends
Because this story of a Mother and a Child
Never is told with the stars left out?

Is it a Holy Night now when a child issues
Out of the dark and the unknown
Into the starlight?

    Down a Winter evening sky
    when a woman hovers
    between two great doorways,

between entry and exit,
between pain to be laughed at,
joy to be wept over—
do the silver-white lines
then come from holy stars?
shall the Newcomer, the Newborn,
be given soft flannels,
swaddling-cloths called Holy?

Shall all wanderers over the earth, all homeless ones,
All against whom doors are shut and words spoken—

Shall these find the earth less strange tonight?
Shall they hear news, a whisper on the night wind?
"A Child is born." "The meek shall inherit the earth."
"And they crucified Him . . . they spat upon Him.
And He rose from the dead."

Shall a quiet dome of stars high over
Make signs and a friendly language
Among all the nations?

Shall they yet gather with no clenched fists at all,
And look into each other's faces and see eye to eye,
And find ever new testaments of man as a sojourner
And a toiler and a brother of fresh understandings?

Shall there be now always
believers and more believers
of sunset and moonrise,
of moonset and dawn,

of wheeling numbers of stars,
and wheels within wheels?

Shall plain habitations off the well-known roads
Count now for a little more than they used to?

Shall plain ways and people held close to earth
be reckoned among things to be written about?

Shall tumult, grandeur, fanfare, panoply, prepared
    loud noises
Stand equal to a quiet heart, thoughts, vast dreams
Of men conquering the earth by conquering
    themselves?
Is there a time for ancient genius of man
To be set for comparison with the latest generations?
Is there a time for stripping to simple, childish
    questions?

On a Holy night we may say:
The Creator of night and of birth
was the Maker of the stars.

—CARL SANDBURG

*When they saw the star, they rejoiced with exceeding
great joy. And when they were come into the house,
they saw the young child with Mary His mother, and
fell down, and worshipped Him: and when they had*

opened their treasures, they presented unto Him gifts;
gold, and frankincense, and myrrh.

MATTHEW 2:10–11

Christmas Star

It was winter.
The wind blew from the steppes.
The child was cold
In the grotto on the slope of a hill.

The breath of an ox comforted him.
Calves and sheep
Crowded together in the cave.
A warm mist hung over the manger.

At midnight on a stony outcrop,
Shepherds shook chaff from their shaggy capes
And grains from their straw bedding.
They looked drowsily into the distance.

Far off were fields and fences,
And village headstones covered with snow,
And cart-shafts deep in a snow drift.
Above the headstones, the sky was full of stars.

Among them, unseen until now,
More dimly lit than an oil lamp

Hung in a watchman's window,
A Star shone on the road to Bethlehem.

It rose in the sky like a haystack aflame,
Of fiery straw and thatch.
All creation shuddered in awe,
Astonished by this new Star.

Its scarlet nimbus grew wider and deeper—
A portent for all to see;
Three stargazers saw the blaze from afar;
They hurried after its beckoning light.

Their camels were laden with gifts.
Their saddled donkeys, sure-footed and tiny,
Trod in little steps down the hills.

In the misty dawn, as gray as ash,
Draymen and shepherds stamped their feet.
Footmen squabbled with horsemen.
By a water-trough in a hollowed log,
Camels bellowed and asses brayed.

There was light. Dawn swept the final stars
From heaven's arch like specks of ash.
From the teeming rabble, the Magi alone
Mary allowed to enter the hillside grotto.

He slept in the oaken manger, aglow with light,
Like a moonbeam in the cleft of a tree.

The warm breath from an ox and an ass
Enveloped him, as if in a sheepskin robe.

The Magi stood in the shadowy den;
They whispered in stammering words.
Suddenly, from the dark, they were nudged
To move a little aside from the manger;
They looked around; like a guest at the threshold.
The Christmas Star gazed upon the Maid.

—BORIS PASTERNAK

But Mary kept all these things, and pondered them in her heart.

LUKE 2:19

The Virgin Mary to the Child Jesus

Sleep, sleep mine Holy One!
My flesh, my Lord!—what name? I do not know
A name that seemeth not too high or low,
Too far from me or heaven.

My Jesus, that is best! that word being given
By the majestic angel whose command
Was softly as a man's beseeching said,

When I and all the earth appeared to stand
    In the great overflow
Of light celestial from his wings and head.
Sleep, sleep, my saving One!

And art Thou come for saving, baby-browed
And speechless Being—art Thou come for saving?
The palm that grown beside our door is bowed
By treadings of the low wind from the south,
A restless shadow through the chamber waving:
Upon its bough a bird sings in the sun;
But Thou, with that close slumber on thy mouth,
Dost seem of wind and sun already weary.
Art come for saving, O my weary One?

Perchance this sleep that shutteth out the dreary
Earth-sounds and motion, opens on Thy soul
    High dreams on fire with God;
High sounds that make the pathways where they roll
More bright than stars do theirs; and visions new
Of thine eternal Nature's old abode.
    Suffer this mother's kiss.
    Best thing that earthly is,
To glide the music and the glory through,
Nor narrow in Thy dream the broad upliftings
    Of any seraph wing.
Thus noiseless, thus. Sleep, sleep, my dreaming One!

We sate among the stalls at Bethlehem.
The dumb kine from their fodder turning them,
    Softened their horned faces

To almost human gazes
    Toward the newly Born.
The simple shepherds from the star-lit brooks
    Brought visionary looks,
As yet in their astonished hearing rung
    The strange, sweet angel-tongue:
The magi of the East, in sandals worn,
    Knelt reverent, sweeping round,
With long pale beards, their gifts upon the ground,
    The incense, myrrh, and gold
These baby hands were impotent to hold.
So, let all earthlies and celestials wait
    Upon Thy royal state,
    Sleep, sleep, my kingly One!

—ELIZABETH BARRETT BROWNING

And when eight days were accomplished for the circumcising of the child, His name was called JESUS, which was so named of the angel before He was conceived in the womb.

LUKE 2:21

To His Savior, the New Year's Gift

That little pretty bleeding part
    Of foreskin send to me:
And I'll return a bleeding heart,
    For New-year's gift to thee.

Rich is the gem that thou didst send,
    Mine's faulty too, and small:
But yet this gift Thou wilt commend,
    Because I send Thee all.

—Robert Herrick

Upon the Circumcision

He, who with all Heaven's heraldry whilere
Entered the world, now bleeds to give us ease;
Alas, how soon our sin
    Sore doth begin
        His Infancy to seize!
O more exceeding love or law more just?
Just law indeed, but more exceeding love!
For we by rightful doom remediless
Were lost in death, till he that dwelt above
High-throned in secret bliss, for us frail dust
Emptied his glory, even to nakedness;
And that great Covenant which we still transgress
Entirely satisfied,

And the full wrath beside
Of vengeful Justice bore for our excess,
And seals obedience first with wounding smart
This day; but Oh! ere long
Huge pangs and strong
  Will pierce more near his heart.

—John Milton

Now when Jesus was born in Bethlehem of Judaea in the days of Herod the king, behold, there came wise men from the east to Jerusalem, Saying, Where is he that is born King of the Jews? for we have seen his star in the east, and are come to worship him. When Herod the king had heard these things, he was troubled, and all Jerusalem with him. And when he had gathered all the chief priests and scribes of the people together, he demanded of them where Christ should be born. And they said unto him, In Bethlehem of Judaea: for thus it is written by the prophet, And thou Bethlehem, in the land of Judah, art not the least among the princes of Judah: for out of thee shall come a Governor, that shall rule my people Israel. Then Herod, when he had privily called the wise men, inquired of them diligently what time the star appeared. And he sent them to Bethlehem, and said, Go and search diligently for the young child; and when ye have found him, bring me word again, that I may come and

34

worship him also. When they had heard the king, they departed; and, lo, the star, which they saw in the east, went before them, till it came and stood over where the young child was. When they saw the star, they rejoiced with exceeding great joy. And when they were come into the house, they saw the young child with Mary His mother, and fell down, and worshipped Him: and when they had opened their treasures, they presented unto Him gifts; gold, and frankincense, and myrrh. And being warned of God in a dream that they should not return to Herod, they departed into their own country another way.

MATTHEW 2:1—12

The Journey of the Magi

"A cold coming we had of it,
Just the worst time of the year
For a journey, and such a long journey:
The ways deep and the weather sharp,
The very dead of winter."
And the camels galled, sore-footed, refractory,
Lying down in the melting snow.
There were times we regretted
The summer palaces on slopes, the terraces,
And the silken girls bringing sherbet.
Then the camel men cursing and grumbling

And running away, and wanting their liquor and
    women,
And the night-fires going out, and the lack of shelters,
And the cities hostile and the towns unfriendly
And the villages dirty and charging high prices:
A hard time we had of it.
At the end we preferred to travel all night,
Sleeping in snatches,
With the voices singing in our ears, saying
That this was all folly.
Then at dawn we came down to a temperate valley,
Wet, below the snow line, smelling of vegetation,
With a running stream and a water-mill beating the
    darkness,
And three trees on the low sky.
And an old white horse galloped away in the meadow.
Then we came to a tavern with vine-leaves over the
    lintel,
Six hands at an open door dicing for pieces of silver,
And feet kicking the empty wine-skins.
But there was no information, and so we continued
And arrived at evening, not a moment too soon
Finding the place; it was (you may say) satisfactory.

As this was a long time ago, I remember,
And I would do it again, but set down
This set down
This; were we led all that way for
Birth or Death? There was a Birth, certainly,
We had evidence and no doubt. I had seen birth and
    death,

But had thought they were different; this Birth was
Hard and bitter agony for us, like Death, our death.
We returned to our places, these Kingdoms,
But no longer at ease here, in the old dispensation,
With an alien people clutching their gods.
I should be glad of another death.

—T. S. Eliot

The Three Kings

Three Kings came riding from far away,
    Melchior and Gaspar and Balthasar;
Three Wise Men out of the East were they.
And they traveled by night and they slept by day,
    For their guide was a beautiful, wonderful star.

The star was so beautiful, large, and clear,
    That all the other stars of the sky
Became a white mist in the atmosphere,
And by this they knew that the coming was near
    Of the Prince foretold in the prophecy.

Three caskets they bore on their saddle-bows,
    Three caskets of gold with golden keys;
Their robes were of crimson silk with rows
Of bells and pomegranates and furbelows,
    Their turbans like blossoming almond-trees.

And so the Three Kings rode into the West,
      Through the dusk of night, over hill and dell,
And sometimes they nodded with beard on breast,
And sometimes talked, as they paused to rest,
      With the people they met at some wayside well.

"Of the child that is born," said Balthasar,
      "Good people, I pray you, tell us the news;
For we in the East have seen his star,
And have ridden fast, and have ridden far,
      To find and worship the king of the Jews."

And the people answered, "You ask in vain;
      We know of no king but Herod the Great!"
They thought the Wise Men were men insane,
As they spurred their horses across the plain,
      Like riders in haste, and who cannot wait.

And when they came to Jerusalem,
      Herod the Great, who had heard this thing,
Sent for the Wise Men and questioned them;
And said, "Go down unto Bethlehem,
      And bring me tidings of this new king."

So they rode away; and the star stood still,
      The only one in the gray of morn;
Yes, it stopped,—it stood still of its own free will,
Right over Bethlehem on the hill,
      The city of David, where Christ was born.

And the Three Kings rode through the gate and guard,
    Through the silent street, till their horses turned
And neighed as they entered the great inn-yard;
But the windows were closed, and the doors were
    barred,
    And only a light in the stable burned.

And cradled there in the scented hay,
    In the air made sweet by the breath of kine,
The little child in the manger lay,
The child, that would be king one day
    Of a kingdom not human but divine.

His mother Mary of Nazareth
    Sat watching beside his place of rest,
Watching the even flow of his breath,
For the joy of life and the terror of death
    Were mingled together in her breast.

They laid their offerings at his feet:
    The gold was their tribute to a King,
The frankincense, with its odor sweet,
Was for the Priest, the Paraclete,
    The myrrh for the body's burying.

And the mother wondered and bowed her head,
    And sat as still as a statue of stone;
Her heart was troubled yet comforted,
Remembering what the Angel had said
    Of an endless reign and of David's throne.

Then the Kings rode out of the city gate,
With a clatter of hoofs in proud array;
But they went not back to Herod the Great,
For they knew his malice and feared his hate,
And returned to their homes by another way.

—HENRY WADSWORTH LONGFELLOW

And when they were departed, behold, the angel of the Lord appeareth to Joseph in a dream, saying, Arise, and take the young child and His mother, and flee into Egypt, and be thou there until I bring thee word: for Herod will seek the young child to destroy Him. When he arose, he took the young child and His mother by night, and departed into Egypt: And was there until the death of Herod: that it might be fulfilled which was spoken of the Lord by the prophet, saying, Out of Egypt have I called my son. Then Herod, when he saw that he was mocked of the wise men, was exceeding wroth, and sent forth, and slew all the children that were in Bethlehem, and in all the coasts thereof, from two years old and under, according to the time which he had diligently inquired of the wise men.

MATTHEW 2:13—16

The Flight into Egypt

From time to time there are auctions of the fittings that made up the old Dime Museums, and at such an auction you should be able to pick up a revolving cyclorama of the Holy Land and Egypt, which is the scenery for this piece. Turn down the gaslights, for it is night in Palestine, and introduce a lady and a child on a donkey. They are accompanied by an old man on foot. The Donkey's name is HEPZIBAH.

HEPZIBAH. [*For the tenth time*] I'm tired.

OUR LADY. I know, I know.

HEPZIBAH. I'm willing to carry you as far and as fast as I can, but within reason.

ST. JOSEPH. If you didn't talk so much, you'd have more strength for the journey.

HEPZIBAH. It's not my lungs that are tired, it's my legs. When I talk I don't notice how tired I am.

OUR LADY. Do as you think best, Hepzibah, but do keep moving. I can still hear Herod's soldiers behind us.

[*Noise of ironmongery in the wings, right.*]

HEPZIBAH. Well, I'm doing my best.

[*Silence. The Tigris passes on the cyclorama.*]

We must talk or I'll have to halt. We talked over the Romans and the whole political situation, and I must say again that I and every thinking person can only view such a situation with alarm, with real alarm. We talked over the village, and I don't think there's anything more to say about that. Did I remember to tell you that Issachar's daughter's engagement had been broken?

OUR LADY. Yes.

HEPZIBAH. Well, there's always ideas. I hope I can say honestly that I am at home in ideas of all sorts. For instance, back in the yard I'm the leader of a group. Among the girls. Very interesting religious discussions, I can tell you. Very helpful.

ST. JOSEPH. [*As some more iron is heard falling in Judea; the Euphrates passes.*] Can't you hurry a bit?

HEPZIBAH. I always say to the girls: Girls, even in faith we are supposed to use our reason. No one is intended to swallow hook, line and sinker, as the saying is. Now take these children that Herod is killing. Why were they born, since they must die so soon? Can anyone answer that? Or put it another way: Why is the little boy in your arms being saved while the others must perish?

ST. JOSEPH. Is it necessary to stop?

HEPZIBAH. I was stopping for emphasis. Mind you, it's not that I doubt. Honest discussion does not imply doubt necessarily. What was that noise?

OUR LADY. I beg of you to make all the haste you can. The noise you hear is that of Herod's soldiers. My child will be slain while you argue about faith. I beg of you, Hepzibah, to save him while you can.

HEPZIBAH. I assure you I'm doing the best I can, and I think I'm moving along smartly. I didn't mean that noise, anyway; it was a noise ahead. Of course, your child is dearer to you than others, but theologically speaking, there's no possible reason why you should escape safely into Egypt while the others should be put to the sword as the Authorized Version has it. When the Messiah comes these things will be made clear, but until then I intend to exercise my reasoning faculty. My theory is this . . .

OUR LADY. Hepzibah, we shall really have to beat you if you stop so often. Hepzibah, don't you remember me? Don't you remember how you fell on your knees in the stable? Don't you remember my child?

HEPZIBAH. What? What! Of course!

OUR LADY. Yes, Hepzibah.

HEPZIBAH. Let me stop just a moment and look around. No, I don't dare to stop. Why didn't I recognize you before! Really, my lady, you should have spoken more sharply to me. I didn't know I could run like this; it's a pleasure. Lord, what a donkey I was to be arguing about reason while my Lord was in danger.

[*A pyramid flies by.*]

Do you see the lights of the town yet? That's the Sphinx at the right, madam, yes, 3655 B.C. Well, well, it's a queer world where the survival of the Lord is dependent upon donkeys, but so it is. Why didn't you tell me before, my lady?

ST. JOSEPH. We thought you could carry us forward on your own merit.

HEPZIBAH. Oh, forgive me, madam; forgive

me, sir. You don't hear any more soldiers now, I
warrant you. Please don't direct me so far—excuse
me—to the right, madam. That's the Nile, and there
are crocodiles. My lady, may I ask one question
now that we're safe?

OUR LADY. Yes, Hepzibah.

HEPZIBAH. It's this matter of faith and reason, madam. I'd love to carry back to our group of
girls whatever you might say about it . . .

OUR LADY. Dear Hepzibah, perhaps some
day. For the present just do as I do and bear your
master on.

[*More pyramids fly by; Memnon sings; the Nile
moves dreamily past, and the inn is reached.*]

—THORNTON WILDER

The Holy Innocents

Listen, the hay-bells tinkle as the cart
Wavers on rubber tires along the tar
And cindered ice below the burlap mill
And ale-wife run. The oxen drool and start
In wonder at the fenders of a car
And blunder hugely up St. Peter's hill.
These are undefiled by women—their
Sorrow is not the sorrow of this world:
King Herod shrieking vengeance at the curled
Up knees of Jesus choking in the air,

A king of speechless clods and infants. Still
The world out-Herods Herod; and the year,
The nineteen-hundred forty-fifth of grace,
Lumbers with losses up the clinkered hill
Of our purgations; and the oxen near
The worn foundations of their resting place,
The holy manger where their bed is corn
And holly torn for Christmas. If they die,
As Jesus, in the harness, who will mourn?
Lamb of the shepherds, Child, how still you lie.

—ROBERT LOWELL

To the Infant Martyrs

Go smiling souls, your new built cages break,
In Heaven you'll learn to sing ere here to speak,
Nor let the milky fonts that bathe your thirst,
    Be your delay;
The place that calls you hence, is at the worst
    Milk all the way.

—RICHARD CRASHAW

And when the days of her purification according to the law of Moses were accomplished, they brought Him to Jerusalem, to present Him to the Lord; (As it is written in the law of the LORD, Every male that openeth the womb shall be called holy to the Lord;) And to offer a sacrifice according to that which is said in the law of the Lord, A pair of turtledoves, or two young pigeons. And, behold, there was a man in Jerusalem, whose name was Simeon; and the same man was just and devout, waiting for the consolation of Israel: and the Holy Ghost was upon him. And it was revealed unto him by the Holy Ghost, that he should not see death, before he had seen the Lord's Christ. And he came by the Spirit into the temple: and when the parents brought in the child Jesus, to do for Him after the custom of the law, Then took he Him up in his arms, and blessed God, and said, Lord, now lettest thou Thy servant depart in peace, according to thy word: For mine eyes have seen Thy salvation, Which Thou hast prepared before the face of all people; A light to lighten the Gentiles, and the glory of thy people Israel. And Joseph and His mother marvelled at those things which were spoken of Him. And Simeon blessed them, and said unto Mary His mother, Behold, this child is set for the fall and rising again of many in Israel; and for a sign which shall be spoken against; (Yea, a sword shall pierce through thy own soul also,) that the thoughts of many hearts may be revealed. And there was one

Anna, a prophetess, the daughter of Phanuel, of the tribe of Aser: she was of a great age, and had lived with an husband seven years from her virginity; And she was a widow of about fourscore and four years, which departed not from the temple, but served God with fastings and prayers night and day. And she coming in that instant gave thanks likewise unto the Lord, and spake of Him to all them that looked for redemption in Jerusalem. And when they had performed all things according to the law of the Lord, they returned into Galilee, to their own city Nazareth.

LUKE 2:22—39

A Song for Simeon

Lord, the Roman hyacinths are blooming in bowls
  and
The winter sun creeps by the snow hills;
The stubborn season has made stand.
My life is light, waiting for the death wind,
Like a feather on the back of my hand.
Dust in sunlight and memory in corners
Wait for the wind that chills towards the dead land.

Grant us thy peace.
I have walked many years in this city,

Kept faith and fast, provided for the poor,
Have given and taken honour and ease.
There went never any rejected from my door.
Who shall remember my house, where shall live my
    children's children
When the time of sorrow is come?
They will take to the goat's path, and the fox's home,
Fleeing from the foreign faces and the foreign swords.

Before the time of cords and scourges and lamentation
Grant us thy peace.
Before the stations of the mountain of desolation,
Before the certain hour of maternal sorrow,
Now at this birth season of decease,
Let the Infant, the still unspeaking and unspoken
    Word,
Grant Israel's consolation
To one who has eighty years and no tomorrow.

According to thy word.
They shall praise Thee and suffer in every generation
With glory and derision,
Light upon light, mounting the saints' stair.
Not for me the martyrdom, the ecstasy of thought
    and prayer,
Not for me the ultimate vision.
Grant me thy peace.
    (And a sword shall pierce thy heart,
Thine also.)
I am tired with my own life and the lives of those
    after me,

I am dying in my own death and the deaths of those
    after me.
Let thy servant depart,
Having seen thy salvation.

—T. S. ELIOT

*Now His parents went to Jerusalem every year at
the feast of the passover. And when He was twelve
years old, they went up to Jerusalem after the custom of the feast. And when they had fulfilled the
days, as they returned, the child Jesus tarried behind
in Jerusalem; and Joseph and His mother knew not
of it. But they, supposing Him to have been in the
company, went a day's journey; and they sought
Him among their kinsfolk and acquaintance. And
when they found Him not, they turned back again
to Jerusalem, seeking Him. And it came to pass, that
after three days they found Him in the temple, sitting in the midst of the doctors, both hearing them,
and asking them questions. And all that heard Him
were astonished at His understanding and answers.
And when they saw Him, they were amazed: and his
mother said unto Him, Son, why hast thou thus
dealt with us? behold, thy father and I have sought
Thee sorrowing. And He said unto them, How is it
that ye sought Me? wist ye not that I must be about
My Father's business? And they understood not the
saying which He spake unto them.*

LUKE 2:41—50

After Three Days

    I stood within the gate
Of a great temple, 'mid the living stream
Of worshippers that thronged its regal state
    Fair-pictured in my dream.

    Jewels and gold were there;
And floors of marble lent a crystal sheen
To body forth, as in a lower air,
    The wonders of the scene.

    Such wild and lavish grace
Had whispers in it of a coming doom;
As richest flowers lie strown about the face
    Of her that waits the tomb.

    The wisest of the land
Had gathered there, three solemn trysting-days,
For high debate: men stood on either hand
    To listen and to gaze.

    The aged brows were bent,
Bent to a frown, half thought, and half annoy,
That all their stores of subtlest argument
    Were baffled by a boy.

    In each averted face
I marked but scorn and loathing, till mine eyes
Fell upon one that stirred not in his place,
    Tranced in a dumb surprise.

Surely within his mind
Strange thoughts are born, until he doubts the lore
Of those old men, blind leaders of the blind,
    Whose kingdom is no more.

Surely he sees afar
A day of death the stormy future brings;
The crimson setting of the herald-star
    That led the Eastern kings.

Thus, as a sunless deep
Mirrors the shining heights that crown the bay,
So did my soul create anew in sleep
    The picture seen by day.

Gazers came and went—
A restless hum of voices marked the spot—
In varying shades of critic discontent
    Prating they knew not what.

"Where is the comely limb,
The form attuned in every perfect part,
The beauty that we should desire in him?"
    Ah! Fools and slow of heart!

Look into those deep eyes,
Deep as the grave, and strong with love divine;
Those tender, pure, and fathomless mysteries
    That seem to pierce through thine.

Look into those deep eyes,
Stirred to unrest by breath of coming strife,
Until a longing in thy soul arise
    That this indeed were life:

    That thou couldst find Him there,
Bend at His sacred feet thy willing knee,
And from thy heart pour out the passionate prayer,
    "Lord, let me follow thee!"

    But see the crowd divide:
Mother and sire have found their lost one now;
The gentle voice, that fain would seem to chide,
    Whispers, "Son, why hast thou"—

    In tone of sad amaze—
"Thus dealt with us, that art our dearest thing?
Behold, thy sire and I, three weary days,
    Have sought thee sorrowing."

    And I had stayed to hear
The loving words, "How is it that ye sought?"—
But that the sudden lark, with matins clear,
    Severed the links of thought.

    Then over all there fell
Shadow and silence; and my dream was fled,
As fade the phantoms of a wizard's cell
    When the dark charm is said.

    Yet, in the gathering light,
I lay with half-shut eyes that would not wake,
Lovingly clinging to the skirts of night
    For that sweet vision's sake.

                    —Lewis Carroll

Jesus in the Temple

With His Kind mother, who partakes thy woe,
Joseph, turn back; see where your Child doth sit,
Blowing, yea blowing out those sparks of wit
Which Himself on the doctors did I bestow.
The Word but lately could not speak, and lo!
It suddenly speaks wonders; whence comes it
That all which was, and all which should be writ,
A shallow-seeming child should deeply know?
His Godhead was not soul to His manhood,
Not had time mellow'd Him to this ripeness;
But as for one which hath a long task, 'tis good,
With the sun to begin His business,
He in His age's morning thus began,
By miracles exceeding power of man.

                    —John Donne

Child

The young child, Christ, is straight and wise
And asks questions of the old men, questions
Found under running water for all children,
And found under shadows thrown on still waters
by tall trees looking downwards, old and gnarled,
Found to the eyes of children alone, untold,
Singing a low song in the loneliness.
And the young child, Christ, goes asking
And the old men answer nothing and only know love
For the young child, Christ, straight and wise.

—CARL SANDBURG

THE MINISTRY

In those days came John the Baptist, preaching in the wilderness of Judaea, And saying, Repent ye: for the kingdom of heaven is at hand. For this is he that was spoken of by the prophet Esaias, saying, The voice of one crying in the wilderness, Prepare ye the way of the Lord, make His paths straight. And the same John had his raiment of camel's hair, and a leathern girdle about his loins; and his meat was locusts and wild honey. Then went out to him Jerusalem, and all Judaea, and all the region round about Jordan, And were baptized of him in Jordan, confessing their sins. But when he saw many of the Pharisees and Sadducees come to his baptism, he said unto them, O generation of vipers, who hath warned you to flee from the wrath to come? Bring forth therefore fruits meet for repentance: And think not to say within yourselves, We have Abraham to our father: for I say unto you, that

God is able of these stones to raise up children unto Abraham. And now also the axe is laid unto the root of the trees: therefore every tree which bringeth not forth good fruit is hewn down, and cast into the fire. I indeed baptize you with water unto repentance: but He that cometh after me is mightier than I, whose shoes I am not worthy to bear: He shall baptize you with the Holy Ghost, and with fire: Whose fan is in His hand, and He will throughly purge His floor, and gather His wheat into the garner; but He will burn up the chaff with unquenchable fire.

MATTHEW 3:1—12

John the Baptist

*W*hen Jesus was thirty years old he heard of people going to hear a holy man preach in the wilderness. This man's name was John. So Jesus went into the wilderness with others, to hear John preach.

John said it was time for the Kingdom of God to come, when everyone will understand that all men are equal and that no one is higher and no one lower than another, and that all men should live lovingly and in good accord with their fellows. He said this time was near, but would only quite come when people stopped doing wrong.

When plain people asked him: "What am I to

do?" John told them that he who had two garments should give one to him who had none, and in the same way he that had food should share it with him that had none. To the rich, John said that they should not rob the people. The soldiers he told not to plunder, but to be content with what was given them, and not to use bad language. The Pharisees and Sadducees, the lawyers, he told to change their lives and to repent: "Do not think," he said to them, "that you are some special kind of men. Change your lives and change them so that men may see by your actions that you have changed. If you do not change you will not escape the fate of the fruit-tree that bears no fruit. If the tree bears no fruit it is cut down for firewood, and that is what will happen to you if you do no good. If you do not alter your lives you will perish."

John tried to persuade everyone to be merciful, just, and meek. And those who promised to amend their lives he bathed in the river Jordan as a sign of the change in their lives. And when he bathed them he said: "I cleanse you with water, but only the spirit of God within you can make you quite pure."

—Leo Tolstoy

Now when all the people were baptized, it came to pass, that Jesus also being baptized, and praying, the heaven was opened, And the Holy Ghost

descended in a bodily shape like a dove upon Him,
and a voice came from heaven, which said, Thou
art My beloved Son; in Thee I am well pleased.

LUKE 3:21—22

The Waterfall

Dear stream, dear bank, where often I
Have sat, and pleased my pensive eye,
Why, since each drop of thy quick store
Runs thither, whence it flowed before,
Should poor souls fear a shade or night,
Who came, sure, from a sea of light?
Or since those drops are all sent back
So sure to thee, that none doth lack,
Why should frail flesh doubt any more
That what God takes, he'll not restore?

O useful Element and clear!
My sacred wash and cleanser here,
My first consigner unto those
Fountains of life, where the Lamb goes,
What sublime truths, and wholesome themes
Lodge in thy mystical, deep streams!
Such as dull man can never find,
Unless that Spirit lead his mind
Which first upon thy face did move,
And hatched all with his quickening love.

As this loud brook's incessant fall
In streaming rings restagnates all,
Which reach by course the bank, and then
Are no more seen, just so pass men.

O my invisible estate,
My glorious liberty, still late!
Thou art the channel my soul seeks,
Not this with cataracts and creeks.

—Henry Vaughan

Heaven Opened

Now had the great Proclaimer, with a voice
More awful than the sound of trumpet, cried
Repentance, and heaven's kingdom nigh at hand
To all baptized: to His great baptism flocked
With awe the regions round, and with them came
From Nazareth the son of Joseph deemed
To the flood Jordan, came, as then obscure,
Unmarked, unknown; but Him the Baptist soon
Descried, divinely warned, and witness bore
As to His worthier, and would have resigned
To Him his heavenly office, nor was long
His witness unconfirmed: on Him baptized
Heaven opened, and in likeness of a dove
The Spirit descended, while the Father's voice
From Heaven pronounced Him His beloved Son.

—John Milton

*And Jesus being full of the Holy Ghost returned
from Jordan, and was led by the Spirit into the
wilderness, Being forty days tempted of the devil.
And in those days He did eat nothing: and when
they were ended, He afterward hungered.*

LUKE 4:1—2

In the Wilderness

Christ of his gentleness
Thirsting and hungering
Walked in the wilderness;
Soft words of grace he spoke
Unto lost desert-folk
That listened wondering.
He heard the bitterns call
From ruined palace-wall,
Answered them brotherly.
He held communion
With the she-pelican
Of lonely piety.
Basilisk, cockatrice,
Flocked to his homilies,
With mail of dread device,
With monstrous barbed stings,
With eager dragon-eyes;
Great rats on leather wings
And poor blind broken things,

Foul in their miseries.
And ever with him went,
Of all his wanderings
Comrade, with ragged coat,
Gaunt ribs—poor innocent—
Bleeding foot, burning throat,
The guileless old scapegoat;
For forty nights and days
Followed in Jesus' ways,
Sure guard behind him kept,
Tears like a lover wept.

—ROBERT GRAVES

Then Jesus turned, and saw them following, and saith unto them, What seek ye? They said unto Him, Rabbi, (which is to say, being interpreted, Master,) where dwellest Thou? He saith unto them, Come and see. They came and saw where He dwelt, and abode with Him that day: for it was about the tenth hour.

JOHN 1:38–39

The Dwelling Place

What happy, secret fountain,
Fair shade, or mountain,
Whose undiscover'd virgin glory
Boasts it this day, though not in story,
Was then Thy dwelling? did some cloud,
Fix'd to a tent, descend and shroud
My distress'd Lord? or did a star,
Beckon'd by Thee, though high and far,
In sparkling smiles haste gladly down
To lodge light, and increase her own?
My dear, dear God! I do not know
What lodg'd Thee then, nor where, nor how;
But I am sure Thou dost now come
Oft to a narrow, homely room,
Where Thou too hast put the least part;
My God, I mean my sinful heart.

—HENRY VAUGHAN

And the third day there was a marriage in Cana of Galilee; and the mother of Jesus was there: And both Jesus was called, and His disciples, to the marriage. And when they wanted wine, the mother of Jesus saith unto him, They have no wine. Jesus saith unto her, Woman, what have I to do with thee? mine hour is not yet come. His mother saith unto the servants, Whatsoever He saith unto you,

do it. *And there were set there six waterpots of stone, after the manner of the purifying of the Jews, containing two or three firkins apiece. Jesus saith unto them, Fill the waterpots with water. And they filled them up to the brim. And He saith unto them, Draw out now, and bear unto the governor of the feast. And they bare it. When the ruler of the feast had tasted the water that was made wine, and knew not whence it was: (but the servants which drew the water knew;) the governor of the feast called the bridegroom, And saith unto him, Every man at the beginning doth set forth good wine; and when men have well drunk, then that which is worse: but thou hast kept the good wine until now. This beginning of miracles did Jesus in Cana of Galilee, and manifested forth His glory; and His disciples believed on him.*

JOHN 2:1—11

Cana

Once when our eyes were clean as noon, our rooms
Filled with the joys of Cana's feast:
For Jesus came, and His disciples, and His Mother,
And after them the singers
And some men with violins.

Once when our minds were Galilees,
And clean as skies our faces,
Our simple rooms were charmed with sun.

GOSPEL

Our thoughts went in and out in whiter coats than
    God's disciples',
In Cana's crowded rooms, at Cana's tables.

Nor did we seem to fear the wine would fail:
For ready, in a row, to fill with water
and a miracle,
We saw our earthen vessels, waiting empty.
What wine those humble waterjars foretell!

Wine for the ones who, bended to the dirty earth,
Have feared, since lovely Eden, the sun's fire,
Yet hardly mumble, in their dusty mouths,
one prayer.

Wine for old Adam, digging in the briars!

—THOMAS MERTON

*And He must needs go through Samaria. Then
cometh He to a city of Samaria, which is called
Sychar, near to the parcel of ground that Jacob gave
to his son Joseph. Now Jacob's well was there. Jesus
therefore, being wearied with His journey, sat thus
on the well: and it was about the sixth hour. There
cometh a woman of Samaria to draw water: Jesus
saith unto her, Give Me to drink. (For His disciples
were gone away unto the city to buy meat.) Then
saith the woman of Samaria unto Him, How is it*

that thou, being a Jew, askest drink of me, which am a woman of Samaria? for the Jews have no dealings with the Samaritans. Jesus answered and said unto her, If thou knewest the gift of God, and who it is that saith to thee, Give me to drink; thou wouldest have asked of Him, and He would have given thee living water. The woman saith unto Him, Sir, thou hast nothing to draw with, and the well is deep: from whence then hast Thou that living water? Art Thou greater than our father Jacob, which gave us the well, and drank thereof himself, and his children, and his cattle? Jesus answered and said unto her, Whosoever drinketh of this water shall thirst again: But whosoever drinketh of the water that I shall give him shall never thirst; but the water that I shall give him shall be in him a well of water springing up into everlasting life. The woman saith unto him, Sir, give me this water, that I thirst not, neither come hither to draw. Jesus saith unto her, Go, call thy husband, and come hither. The woman answered and said, I have no husband. Jesus said unto her, Thou hast well said, I have no husband: For thou hast had five husbands; and he whom thou now hast is not thy husband: in that saidst thou truly. The woman saith unto Him, Sir, I perceive that Thou art a prophet. Our fathers worshipped in this mountain; and ye say, that in Jerusalem is the place where men ought to worship. Jesus saith unto her, Woman, believe me, the hour cometh, when ye shall neither in this mountain, nor yet at Jerusalem, worship the Father. Ye worship ye know not what:

we know what we worship: for salvation is of the Jews. But the hour cometh, and now is, when the true worshippers shall worship the Father in spirit and in truth: for the Father seeketh such to worship Him. God is a Spirit: and they that worship Him must worship Him in spirit and in truth. The woman saith unto him, I know that Messias cometh, which is called Christ: when He is come, He will tell us all things. Jesus saith unto her, I that speak unto thee am He.

JOHN 4:4—26

from *The Woman of Samaria*

(A selection from Edmond Rostand's biblical drama, *La Sameritaine*, written for Sarah Bernhardt.)

JESUS.
    [*PHOTINE is nearly out of sight.*]
O Woman,—I am athirst. The sun is very hot!
Give me to drink, I pray.
    PHOTINE. The Jews deal not,—He is a Jew,
this thirsty, wayworn man,—
With Sichemite or with Samaritan.
Little or large, all dealings they decline.
Our bread, they say, smells of the flesh of swine.
Honey from Sichem hives the Jews refuse;
They say it tastes of blood. My dripping cruise
Came from Samaria's tainted well but now
A heathen bears it on her unclean brow.

You should refuse it, finding it to stink,
Instead of asking for . . .

    JESUS. Give Me to drink!

    PHOTINE. Has your great thirst your teaching
so refuted?
Know, Jew, that you would be the less polluted
Handling foul vermin, reptiles poisonous,
Than being succoured so by one of us.

    [*With quarrelsome volubility.*]
Stay till tomorrow. Either sit or stand.
I'll not let down my pitcher to my hand.
'Tis on my shoulder. There it will remain.
Ho, Eleazar, lacking gifts and train!
I'm not Rebecca, as you seem to think.
Be thirsty if you will. You shall not drink.

    [*Coming back a little way.*]
You see this water,—clear, so pure, so clear,
The cruise seems empty, though I filled it here,
So cool one sees the moisture on the cruise;
Silver and pearl this draught which I refuse.
O Beggar, hear the thirst-provoking sound,
The tinkle, tinkle, in its depths profound,—
Light as a draught distilled of summer air!
No water is so cool, so clear, so fair.
Ah, well for you, the Law, be very sure,
Says that this purest water is impure!

    JESUS. Woman . . .

    PHOTINE. I'd rather pour it on the sod
Than give . . .

    JESUS. If you but knew the gift of God,
And Who brings light when in the dark you shrink—

And Who He is that says Give me to drink;
Who sitteth here upon the well's wide rim,
He would not ask of thee, but thou of Him.

PHOTINE. You speak in riddles just to make
me heed.

JESUS. I would give living waters to thy need.

PHOTINE. Stranger, I listen, for I have no choice,
Some Influence masters me,—your eyes, your voice.
You speak of living waters. Yet you keep
Nothing to draw with, and the well is deep.
Whence hast thou then that water, wondrous Jew?
—It must be false and yet I think it true,—
Is there, in all the sources of Judea,
Water as limpid as this water here?
People an hour away come here to draw,
Our father Jacob built it, when he saw
The land athirst. Here drank his mighty sons,
Their wives, their servants, and their little ones.
Most famous of all famous springs and wells.
What is it this mysterious stranger tells?
Here Jacob's cattle ages since were fed,
Art greater than Jacob?

JESUS. Thou hast said.

PHOTINE. In your cupped hands a little I will
pour. Then you will see . . .

JESUS. He thirsteth nevermore
Whom I have given to drink. With how much pain
You come to draw again and yet again,
But whoso drinks the living draught I give
Within himself shall welling fountains live,
And life eternal from those waters brim,

If he but drink the draught I bring to him.

    PHOTINE. What! For eternity to have no thirst?
A good thing to believe,—if one but durst,
Elijah's draught lasted a wondrous while
While he was in the desert. Ah, you smile?
Some learning to this woman you must grant,—
He went for forty days and did not want.
You've learned his secret in your wandering?
O Master, lead me to that hidden spring.
Show me this wonder, that your wanderings saw,
That I thirst not, nor hither come to draw,

    JESUS. Hearing, thou hearest not, nor givest heed
To any thirst but that of fleshly need.

    PHOTINE. Give me this water. Stranger, I
implore,—
This living water, that I thirst no more.

    JESUS. Go call thy husband and return to Me.
    PHOTINE. My husband?
    JESUS. Go.
    PHOTINE. But I . . . but I
    JESUS. I see, Thou art ashamed.
    PHOTINE. I have no husband.
    JESUS. Verily,
Thou saidest truly. Five men by that name
Were called, and thou wouldst call this sixth the same.

    PHOTINE. Master . . .
    JESUS. Thou saidest truly, yea, and well.
Thou hast no husband, it is truth you tell.
That holy name thou hast no right to speak.

    PHOTINE. Master.
    JESUS. Five men have had thee. Didst thou seek

God's blessings, or the blessing of God's priest?
Troops of young friends and wholesome marriage
      feast?
Torches? . . .

    PHOTINE. O Master.

    JESUS. Merry dulcimer,
Jests gay and tender; tremblings sweet, to stir
The myrtle crown set on thy drooping head? . . .

    PHOTINE. Lord, Lord! a prophet surely, who
hast read . . .

    JESUS. Thou callest Me prophet since I know
thy heart.
It is but part, and such a little part,
If thou wilt learn, of things that I can show.

    PHOTINE. O Master, canst thou tell?

    JESUS. What wouldst thou know?

    PHOTINE. I have lived far from God. I can
receive
Only a little, but I do believe
Three things: the dead will some day come again;
Angels have visited this mortal plain,
And—fairest, surest hope beneath the sun,—
I wait the coming of the Promised One,
Await and love him, *L'Ha-Schaab*, Christ, Messiah!

    JESUS. Hear her, O Father
Woman, have no fear.
Thou sayest the words that I have longed to hear.
Lift up thy head. Behold thy soul's Desire.
I—I that speak—am He. I am Messiah.

                  —EDMOND ROSTAND

And Jesus, walking by the sea of Galilee, saw two brethren, Simon called Peter, and Andrew his brother, casting a net into the sea: for they were fishers. And He saith unto them, Follow Me, and I will make you fishers of men. And they straightway left their nets, and followed Him. And going on from thence, He saw other two brethren, James the son of Zebedee, and John his brother, in a ship with Zebedee their father, mending their nets; and He called them. And they immediately left the ship and their father, and followed Him.

MATTHEW 4:18—22

Jesus to His Disciples

I have instructed you to follow me
What way I go;
The road is hard, and stony,—as I know;
Uphill it climbs, and from the crushing heat
No shelter will be found
Save in my shadow: wherefore follow me; the
    footprints of my feet
Will be distinct and clear;
However trodden on, they will not disappear.

And see ye not at last
How tall I am?—

Even at noon I cast
A shadow like a forest far behind me on the ground.
—EDNA ST. VINCENT MILLAY

The Call of the Four

*T*he first four . . . were poor fishermen, who were sitting in their boats by the seaside, mending their nets, when Christ passed by. He stopped, and went to Simon Peter's boat, and asked him if he had caught many fish. Peter said No; though they had worked all night with their nets, they had caught nothing. Christ said, "Let down the net again." They did so; and it was immediately so full of fish, that it required the strength of many men (who came and helped them) to lift it out of the water, and even then it was very hard to do. This was another of the Miracles of Jesus Christ.

Jesus then said, "Come with me." And they followed Him directly.

—CHARLES DICKENS

Follow Me

*H*e comes to us as One unknown, without a name, as of old, by the lakeside, He came to those men who knew Him not. He speaks to us the same word: "Follow thou me!" and sets us the tasks which He has to fulfill for our time. He commands. And to those who obey Him, whether they be wise or simple, He will reveal Himself in the toils, the conflicts, the sufferings which they will pass through in His fellowship, and, as an ineffable mystery, they shall learn in their own experience Who He is.

—ALBERT SCHWEITZER

After this manner therefore pray ye: Our Father which art in heaven, Hallowed be thy name. Thy kingdom come. Thy will be done in earth, as it is in heaven. Give us this day our daily bread. And forgive us our debts, as we forgive our debtors. And lead us not into temptation, but deliver us from evil: For thine is the kingdom, and the power, and the glory, for ever. Amen.

MATTHEW 6:9—13

Lord's Prayer

Such is the constitution and frame of that Prayer of Prayers, that which is the extraction of all prayers, and draws into a sum all that is in all others, that which is the infusion into all others, sheds and shows whatsoever is acceptable to God, in any other prayer, that prayer which our Saviour gave us, (for as he meant to give us all for asking, so he meant to give us the words by which we should ask). As that prayer consists of seven petitions, and seven is infinite, so by being at first begun with glory and acknowledgement of his reigning in heaven, and then shut up in the same manner, with acclamations of power and glory, it is made a circle of praise, and a circle is infinite too.

—JOHN DONNE

And it came to pass, that, as He was praying in a certain place, when He ceased, one of His disciples said unto him, Lord, teach us to pray, as John also taught his disciples. And He said unto them, When ye pray, say, Our Father which art in heaven, Hallowed be thy name. Thy kingdom come. Thy will be done, as in heaven, so in earth. Give us day by day our daily bread. And forgive us our sins; for we also forgive every one that is indebted to us. And lead us not into temptation; but deliver us from evil.

LUKE 11:1—4

from *Bleak House*

(Allan Woodcourt comforts the poor little crossing sweeper, Jo, on his deathbed.)

After watching him closely a little while, Allan puts his mouth very near his ear, and says to him in a low, distinct voice:

"Jo! Did you ever know a prayer?"

"Never knowd nothing, sir."

"Not so much as one short prayer?"

"No, sir. Nothink at all. Mr. Chadbands he wos a-prayin wunst at Mr. Sangsby's and I heerd him, but he sounded as if he wos a-speakin' to hisself, and not to me. He prayed a lot, but I couldn't make out nothink on it. Different times, there was other genlmen come down Tom-all-Alone's a-prayin, but they all mostly sed as the t'other wuns prayed wrong, and all mostly sounded to be a-talking to theirselves, or a-passing blame on the t'others, and not a-talkin to us. We never knowd nothink. I never knowd what it wos all about."

It takes him a long time to say this; and few but an experienced and attentive listener could hear, or, hearing, understand him.

After a short relapse into sleep or stupor, he makes a sudden and strong effort to get out of bed.

"Stay, Jo! What now?"

"It's time for me to go to that there berryin ground, sir," he returns with a wild look.

"Lie down, and tell me. What burying ground, Jo?"

"Where they laid him as wos wery good to me, wery good to me indeed, he wos. It's time for me to go down to that there berryin ground, sir, and ask to be put along with him. I wants to go there and be berried. He used fur to say to me, 'I am as poor as you today, Jo,' he ses. I wants to tell him that I am as poor as him now, and have come there to be laid along with him."

"By and by, Jo. By and by."

"Ah! P'raps they wouldn't do it if I wos to go myself. But will you promise to have me took there, sir, and laid along with him?"

"I will, indeed."

"Thankee, sir. Thankee, sir. They'll have to get the key of the gate afore they can take me in, for it's allus locked. And there's a step there, as I used for to clean with my broom. It's turned wery dark, sir. Is there any light a-comin?"

"It is coming fast, Jo."

Fast. The cart is shaken all to pieces, and the rugged road is very near its end.

"Jo, my poor fellow!"

"I hear you, sir, in the dark, but I'm a-gropin—a-gropin'—let me catch hold of your hand."

"Jo, can you say what I say?"

"I'll say anythink as you say, sir, fir I know it's good."

"OUR FATHER."

"Our Father!—yes, that's wery good, sir."

"WHICH ART IN HEAVEN."

"Art in heaven—is the light a-comin, sir?"

76

"It is close at hand. HALLOWED BE THY NAME!"

"Hallowed be—thy—"

The light is come upon the dark benighted way. Dead!

—CHARLES DICKENS

After this there was a feast of the Jews; and Jesus went up to Jerusalem. Now there is at Jerusalem by the sheep market a pool, which is called in the Hebrew tongue Bethesda, having five porches. In these lay a great multitude of impotent folk, of blind, halt, withered, waiting for the moving of the water. For an angel went down at a certain season into the pool, and troubled the water: whosoever then first after the troubling of the water stepped in was made whole of whatsoever disease he had. And a certain man was there, which had an infirmity thirty and eight years. When Jesus saw him lie, and knew that he had been now a long time in that case, He saith unto him, Wilt thou be made whole? The impotent man answered him, Sir, I have no man, when the water is troubled, to put me into the pool: but while I am coming, another steppeth down before me. Jesus saith unto him, Rise, take up thy bed, and walk. And immediately the man was made whole, and took up his bed, and walked . . .

JOHN 5:1—9

The Pool of Bethesda

*A*fter this, there was a great feast of the Jews, and Jesus Christ went to Jerusalem. There was, near the sheep market in that place, a pool, or pond, called Bethesda, having five gates to it; and at the time of the year when that feast took place great numbers of sick people and cripples went to this pool to bathe in it: believing that an Angel came and stirred the water, and that whoever went in first after the Angel had done so, was cured of any illness he or she had, whatever it might be. Among those poor persons was one man who had been ill thirty-eight years; and he told Jesus Christ (who took pity on him when He saw him lying on his bed alone, with no one to help him) that he never could be dipped in the pool, because he was so weak and ill that he could not move to get there. Our Saviour said to him, "Take up thy bed and go away." And he went away, quite well.

—CHARLES DICKENS

And He goeth up into a mountain, and calleth unto Him whom He would: and they came unto Him. And He ordained twelve, that they should be with Him, and that He might send them forth to preach, And to have power to heal sicknesses, and to cast out devils: And Simon He surnamed Peter; And

James the son of Zebedee, and John the brother of James; and He surnamed them Boanerges, which is, The sons of thunder: And Andrew, and Philip, and Bartholomew, and Matthew, and Thomas, and James the son of Alphaeus, and Thaddaeus, and Simon the Canaanite, And Judas Iscariot, which also betrayed Him: and they went into an house.

MARK 3:13—19

The Choosing of the Twelve

*T*hat there might be some good men to go about with Him, teaching the people, Jesus Christ chose twelve poor men to be His companions. These twelve are called the "Apostles" or "Disciples," and He chose them from among poor men, in order that the poor might know—always after that, in all years to come—that Heaven was made for them as well as for the rich, and that God makes no difference between those who wear good clothes and those who go barefoot and in rags. The most miserable, the most ugly, deformed, wretched creatures that live, will be bright angels in Heaven if they are good here on earth. Never forget this, when you are grown up. Never be proud or unkind, my dears, to any poor man, woman, or child. If they are bad, think that they would have been better if they had had kind friends, and good homes, and had been

79

better taught. So, always try to make them better by kind persuading words; and always try to teach them and relieve them if you can. And when people speak ill of the poor and miserable, think how Jesus Christ went among them, and taught them, and thought them worthy of His care. And always pity them yourselves, and think as well of them as you can.

—Charles Dickens

And seeing the multitudes, He went up into a mountain: and when He was set, His disciples came unto Him: And He opened His mouth, and taught them . . .

Matthew 5:1—2

Born Again

The Master stood upon the mount, and taught,
He saw a fire in His disciples' eyes:
"The old law," they said, "is wholly come to naught!
    Behold the new world rise!"

"Was it," the Lord then said, "with scorn ye saw
The old law observed by Scribes and Pharisees?
I say unto you, see ye keep that law
    More faithfully than these!

"To hasty heads for ordering worlds, alas!
Think not that I to annul the law have will'd;
No jot, no tittle from the law shall pass,
    Till all hath been fulfill'd."

So Christ said eighteen hundred years ago.
And what then shall be said to those today,
Who cry aloud to lay the old world low
    To clear the new world's way?

"Religious fervours! ardour misapplied!
Hence, hence," they cry, "ye do but keep man blind!
But keep him self-immersed, preoccupied,
    And lame the active mind!"

Ah! from the old world let some one answer give:
"Scorn ye this world, their tears, their inward cares?
I say unto you, see that your souls live
    A deeper life than theirs!
"Say ye: The spirit of man has found new roads,
And we must leave the old faiths, and walk therein?
Leave them the Cross as ye have left carved gods,
    But guard the fire within!

"Bright, else, and fast the stream of life may roll,
And no man may the other's hurt behold:
Yet each will have one anguish—his own soul
    Which perishes of cold."

Here let that voice make end; then let a strain,
From a far lonelier distance, like the wind

Be heard, floating through heaven, and fill again
    These men's profoundest mind:

"Children of men! the unseen Power, whose eye
For ever doth accompany mankind,
Hath looked on no religion scornfully
    That men did ever find.

"Which has not taught weak wills how much they
    can?
Which has not fall'n on the dry heart like rain?
Which has not cried to sunk, self-weary man:
    Thou must be born again!"

—MATTHEW ARNOLD

A Sure Foundation

*N*ow, every now and then, and indeed surprisingly often, Christ finds a word that transcends all commonplace morality; every now and then He quits the beaten track to pioneer the unexpressed, and throws out a pregnant and magnanimous hyperbole; for it is only by some bold poetry of thought that men can be strung up above a level of everyday conceptions to take a broader look upon experience or accept some higher principle of conduct. To a man who is of the same mind that was in Christ, who stands at some centre not too far from His, and looks at the world and conduct from some not dissimilar or, at least, not opposing attitude—or, shortly, to a man who is of Christ's philosophy—every such saying should come home with a thrill of joy and corroboration; he should feel each one below his feet as another sure foundation in the flux of time and chance, each should be another proof that in the torrent of the years and generations, where doctrines and great armaments and empire are swept away and swallowed, he stands immovable, holding by the eternal stars.

—ROBERT LOUIS STEVENSON

Ye are the salt of the earth: but if the salt have lost his savour, wherewith shall it be salted? it is thenceforth good for nothing, but to be cast out, and to be trodden under foot of men. Ye are the light of the world. A city that is set on an hill cannot be hid. Neither do men light a candle, and put it under a bushel, but on a candlestick; and it giveth light unto all that are in the house. Let your light so shine before men, that they may see your good works, and glorify your Father which is in heaven.

MATTHEW 5:13—16

The Candle Indoors

Some candle clear burns somewhere I come by.
I muse at how its being puts blissful back
With yellowy moisture milk night's blear-all black,
Or to-fro tender trambeams truckle at the eye.
By that window what task what fingers ply,
I plod wondering, a-wanting just for lack
Of answer the eagerer a-wanting Jessy or Jack
There God to aggrandise, God to glorify.

Come you indoors, come home; your fading fire
Mend first and vital candle in close heart's vault:
You there are master, do your own desire;
What hinders? Are you beam-blind, yet to a fault
In a neighbour deft-handed? are you that liar
And, cast by conscience out, spendsavour salt?

—GERARD MANLEY HOPKINS

And why take ye thought for raiment? Consider the
lilies of the field, how they grow; they toil not, neither
do they spin: And yet I say unto you, That even
Solomon in all his glory was not arrayed like one of
these.

MATTHEW 6:28—29

Consider

The lilies of the field, whose bloom is brief—
    We are as they;
    Like them we fade away,
        As doth a leaf.

    Consider
The lilies, that do neither spin nor toil,
    Yet are most fair—
    What profits all this care,
        And all this coil?

    Consider
The birds, that have no barn nor harvest-weeks:
    God gives them food—
    Much more our Father seeks
        To do us good.

—CHRISTINA GEORGINA ROSSETTI

Therefore all things whatsoever ye would that men should do to you, do ye even so to them: for this is the law and the prophets.

MATTHEW 7:12

The Greatest Rule

(From a letter Charles Dickens wrote to his youngest son bound for Australia)

Try to do to others as you would have them do to you, and do not be discouraged if they fail sometimes. It is much better for you that they should fail in obeying the greatest rule laid down by our Saviour than that you should. I put a New Testament among your books for the very same reasons, and with the very same hopes, that made me write an easy account of it for you, when you were a little child. Because it is the best book that ever was, or will be, known in the world; and because it teaches you the best lessons by which any human creature, who tries to be truthful and faithful to duty, can possibly be guided. As your brothers have gone away, one by one, I have written to each such words as I am now writing to you, and have entreated them all to guide themselves by this Book, putting aside the interpretations and inventions of Man. You will remember that you have never at home been harassed about religious observances, or mere formalities. I have always been anxious not to weary my children with such things, before they are old enough to form opinions respecting them. You will therefore understand the better that I now most solemnly impress upon you the truth and beauty of the Christian Religion, as it came from Christ Himself, and the impossibility of your going far wrong if you humbly but heartily respect it.

—CHARLES DICKENS

Enter ye in at the strait gate: for wide is the gate, and broad is the way, that leadeth to destruction, and many there be which go in thereat: Because strait is the gate, and narrow is the way, which leadeth unto life, and few there be that find it.

MATTHEW 7:13—14

Baptism II

Since, Lord, to thee
A narrow way and little gate
Is all the passage, on my infancy
Thou didst lay hold, and antedate
My faith in me.

O let me still
Write thee, great God, and me a child:
Let me be soft and supple to thy will,
Small to my self, to others mild,
Be hither ill.

Although by stealth
My flesh get on; yet let her sister
My soul bid nothing, but preserve her wealth:
The growth of flesh is but a blister;
Childhood is health.

—GEORGE HERBERT

*Therefore whosoever heareth these sayings of
Mine, and doeth them, I will liken him unto a wise
man, which built his house upon a rock: And the
rain descended, and the floods came, and the winds
blew, and beat upon that house; and it fell not: for
it was founded upon a rock.*

MATTHEW 7:24—25

A Testimony

I said of laughter: it is vain.
    Of mirth I said: what profits it?
    Therefore I found a book, and writ
Therein how ease and also pain,
How health and sickness, every one
Is vanity beneath the sun.

Our treasures moth and rust corrupt,
    Or thieves break through and steal, or they

Make themselves wings and fly away.
One man made merry as he supped,
Nor guessed how when that night grew dim.
His soul would be required of him.

We build our houses on the sand
    Comely withoutside and within
    But when the winds and rains begin
To beat on them, they cannot stand:
They perish, quickly overthrown,
Loose from the very basement stone.

All things are vanity. I said:
    Yea vanity of vanities.
    The rich man dies; and the poor dies:
The worm feeds sweetly on the dead.
Wheve'er thou lackest, keep the trust:
All in the end shall have but dust:

The one inheritance, which best
    And worst alike shall find and share:
    The wicked cease from troubling there,
And there the weary be at rest;
There all the wisdom of the wise
Is vanity of vanities.

—CHRISTINA GEORGINA ROSSETTI

*My head with oil thou didst not anoint: but this
woman hath anointed My feet with ointment.
Wherefore I say unto thee, Her sins, which are
many, are forgiven; for she loved much: but to
whom little is forgiven, the same loveth little. And
He said unto her, Thy sins are forgiven. And they
that sat at meat with Him began to say within
themselves, Who is this that forgiveth sins also?*

LUKE 7:46—49

Marie Magdalene

When blessed Marie wip'd her Saviour's feet,
(Whose precepts she had trampled on before)
And wore them for a jewel on her head,
 Shewing his steps should be the street,
 Wherein she thenceforth evermore
With pensive humblenesse would live and tread:
She being stain'd herself, why did she strive
To make him clean, who could not be defil'd?
Why kept she not her tears for her own faults?
 And not his feet? Though we could dive
 In tears like seas, our sins are pil'd
Deeper than they, in words, and works, and thoughts.

Dear soul, she knew who did vouchsafe and deign
To bear her filth; and that her sins did dash
Ev'n God himself: wherefore she was not loth,

And she had brought wherewith to stain,
So to bring in wherewith to wash:
And yet in washing one, she washed both.

—George Herbert

And the disciples came, and said unto Him, Why speakest thou unto them in parables? He answered and said unto them, Because it is given unto you to know the mysteries of the kingdom of heaven, but to them it is not given. For whosoever hath, to him shall be given, and he shall have more abundance: but whosoever hath not, from him shall be taken away even that he hath. Therefore speak I to them in parables: because they seeing see not; and hearing they hear not, neither do they understand.

Matthew 13:10—13

On the Holy Scriptures

Why did our blessed Saviour please to break
His sacred thoughts in parables; and speak
In dark enigmas? Whosoe'er thou be
That findst them so, they were not spoke to thee:
In what a case is he, that haps to run
Against a post, and cries, How dark's the sun?

GOSPEL

Or he, in summer, that complains of frost?
The Gospel's hid to none, but who are lost:
The Scripture is a ford, wherein, 'tis said,
An elephant shall swim; a lamb may wade.

—FRANCIS QUARLES

*Another parable put he forth unto them, saying,
The kingdom of heaven is like to a grain of mustard
seed, which a man took, and sowed in his field:
Which indeed is the least of all seeds: but when it is
grown, it is the greatest among herbs, and
becometh a tree, so that the birds of the air come
and lodge in the branches thereof.*

MATTHEW 13:31—32

The Kingdom of Heaven Compared
to a Grain of Mustard-Seed

Then did he to the throng around
Another parable propound.
So fares it with the heavenly reign
As mustard-seed, of which a grain
Was taken in a farmer's hand
And cast into a piece of land.
This grain, the least of all that's sown,

When once to full perfection grown,
Outstrips all herbs to that degree
Till it at length becomes a tree,
And all the songsters of the air
Take up an habitation there.

Christ laid (at first an infant boy)
The basis of eternal joy;
And from humility, his plan,
Arose the best and greatest man,
The greatest man that ever trod
On earth was Christ th'eternal God,
Which as the branch of Jesse's root
Ascends to bear immortal fruit.
From contradiction, sin and strife,
He spreads abroad the tree of life;
And there his servants shall partake
The mansions that the branches make;
There saints innumerable throng,
Assert their seat, and sing their song.

—CHRISTOPHER SMART

He answered and said unto them, He that soweth the good seed is the Son of man; The field is the world; the good seed are the children of the kingdom; but the tares are the children of the wicked one.

MATTHEW 13:37—38

GOSPEL

See How Spring Opens with Disabling Cold

See how Spring opens with disabling cold,
And hunting winds and the long-lying snow.
Is it a wonder if the buds are slow?
Or where is strength to make the leaf unfold?
Chilling remembrance of my days of old
Afflicts no less, what yet I hope may blow,
That seed which the good sower once did sow,
So loading with obstruction that threshold
Which should ere now have led my feet to the field.
It is the waste done in unreticent youth
Which makes so small the promise of that yield
That I may win with late-learnt skill uncouth
From furrows of the poor and stinting weald.
Therefore how bitter, and learnt how late, the truth!

—GERARD MANLEY HOPKINS

Again, the kingdom of heaven is like unto a merchant man, seeking goodly pearls: Who, when he had found one pearl of great price, went and sold all that he had, and bought it.

MATTHEW 13:45—46

The Pearl

I know the ways of learning; both the head
And pipes that feed the press, and make it run;
What reason hath from nature borrowed,
Or of itself, a good housewife, spun
In laws and policy; what the stars conspire,
What willing nature speaks, what forced by fire;
Both th'old discoveries, and the new-found seas,
The stock and surplus, cause and history:
All these stand open, or I have the keys:
      Yet I love thee.

I know the ways of honor, what maintains
The quick returns of courtesy and wit:
In view of favors whether party gains,
When glory swells the heart, and moldeth it
To all expressions both of hand and eye,
Which on the world a true-love-knot may tie,
And bear the bundle, wheresoe'er it goes:
How many drams of spirit there must be
To sell my life unto my friends or foes:
      Yet I love thee.
I know the ways of pleasure, the sweet strains,
The lullings and the relishes of it;
The propositions of hot blood and brains;
What mirth and music mean; what love and wit
Have done these twenty hundred years, and more;
I know the projects of unbridled store:
My stuff is flesh, not brass; my senses live,
And grumble oft, that they have more in me

Than he that curbs them being but one to five:
>Yet I love thee.

I know all these, and have them in my hand:
Therefore not sealed, but with open eyes
I fly to thee, and fully understand
Both the main gale, and the commodities;
And at what rate and price I have thy love;
With all the circumstances that may move:
Yet through the labyrinths, not my groveling wit,
But thy silk twist let down from heaven to me,
Did both conduct and teach me, how by it
>To climb to thee.

—GEORGE HERBERT

And when it was evening, His disciples came to Him, saying, This is a desert place, and the time is now past; send the multitude away, that they may go into the villages, and buy themselves victuals. But Jesus said unto them, They need not depart; give ye them to eat. And they say unto Him, We have here but five loaves, and two fishes. He said, Bring them hither to Me. And He commanded the multitude to sit down on the grass, and took the five loaves, and the two fishes, and looking up to heaven, He blessed, and brake, and gave the loaves to His disciples, and the disciples to the multitude. And they did all eat, and were filled: and they took

up of the fragments that remained twelve baskets full. And they that had eaten were about five thousand men, beside women and children. And straightway Jesus constrained His disciples to get into a ship, and to go before Him unto the other side, while he sent the multitudes away. And when He had sent the multitudes away, He went up into a mountain apart to pray: and when the evening was come, He was there alone.

MATTHEW 14:15—23

Loaves and Fishes

ANDREW. Master, it's getting on towards evening, and the people have got nothing to eat.

JOHN. The children are crying. We don't know what to do with them.

JUDAS. Hadn't we better tell them to go away and buy some food?

JESUS. There's no need for them to go. Give them some of your own food.

SIMON. But that's ridiculous. We haven't enough for all this crowd. Why, there must be three or four thousand of them.

THOMAS. Nearer five thousand, if you ask me.

JESUS. Then you must go and buy some. You go, Philip. Ask Judas for the money.

PHILIP. We'd need two hundred pennyworth of

bread at least. And even then they'd only get a snack apiece.

JUDAS. Two hundred pence! You might as well ask for two hundred pounds! Really we can't.

JESUS. Well, how much food have you got? Go and see.

PHILIP. Master, I've been to see, and there's scarcely anything left. Look!

ANDREW. We've got five barley loaves and two dried fish—rather small ones. But what's the good of them among all this lot?

JESUS. Well, we must do the best and trust to God. Tell the people to sit down—over there, on that smooth slope of green grass. . . . What's the matter now, Thomas Didymus?

THOMAS. (*bluntly*) It seems a bit silly, that's all. But just as you like, of course.

JESUS. Thomas, we could do with a little more faith and rather fewer objections.

MATTHEW. Here, come on, Thomas. Why don't you do as he says? Argue anybody's head off, you would, and don't you know he's always right?

THOMAS. I don't like looking a fool.

MATTHEW. What's it matter what *you* look like? Let's get on with it.

ANDREW. What are we to say to them?

JAMES. Better put a bold face on it . . . Now, you people! The Rabbi knows you've come a long way and you must be tired and hungry. We didn't expect such a large party, and we can't invite you to a banquet—only some bread and fish. But our

Master makes you welcome to what we've got.

(*Murmurs of approval*)

Will you all please sit down over there?

MATTHEW. Here! not all in a bunch like that! Make a nice row here of fifty or so. That's right. Now another row behind—see! . . . Move up a bit, missus—this your youngster? Well, catch hold of him . . . That's famous!

(*Confusion and some laughs*)

DISCIPLES. Another row here. . . . No, a little further back . . . Sit a bit closer. . . . Four, six, eight . . . We can get a hundred in between these two rocks. . . .

JOHN. Master—the people are ready. Shall we serve to them now?

JESUS. Children of Israel. To-day you are my guests, and the guests of my Father's Kingdom.

MAN IN CROWD. Thank-you, good Rabbi. Blessed are they that shall eat bread in the Kingdom of God.

JOHN. Master, will you bless the bread?

JESUS. Father of all goodness, we thank Thee for Thy gifts. Blessed be this bread and meat unto our bodies, as Thy word to our souls. Amen.

DISCIPLES. Amen.

JESUS. Take the food, and distribute it to the people, that every one may eat and be filled.

DISCIPLES. Eat and be filled . . . eat and be filled . . . eat and be filled.

CROWD. Thanks be to God! Blessings on the name of the Prophet. . . .

(*Keep this going while THE EVANGELIST speaks*)

THE EVANGELIST. And they did all eat and were filled. And they took up of the fragments that remained twelve baskets full.

CROWD. A prophet! A prophet! Blessed be Jesus the Prophet! A miracle! The Kingdom is come among us!—A land flowing with milk and honey!—Blessings on the name of Jesus! Blessed be the Prophet of God! Follow the Prophet who feeds his people! A prophet in Israel! Follow him! Follow him! Hail to the Prophet Jesus!

—Dorothy L. Sayers

Now it came to pass on a certain day, that He went into a ship with His disciples: and He said unto them, Let us go over unto the other side of the lake. And they launched forth. But as they sailed He fell asleep: and there came down a storm of wind on the lake; and they were filled with water, and were in jeopardy. And they came to Him, and awoke Him, saying, Master, Master, we perish. Then He arose, and rebuked the wind and the raging of the water: and they ceased, and there was a calm. And He said unto them, Where is your faith? And they being afraid wondered, saying one to another, What manner of man is this! for He commandeth even the winds and water, and they obey Him.

Luke 8:22—25

Walking on the Sea

When the storm on the mountains of Galilee fell,
    And lifted its waters on high;
And the faithless disciples were bound in the spell,
Of mysterious alarm,—their terrors to quell,
    Jesus whispered, "Fear not, it is I."

The storm could not bury that word in the wave,
    For 'twas taught through the tempest to fly;
It shall reach his disciples in every clime,
And his voice shall be near in each troublous time,
    Saying, "Be not afraid, it is I."

When the spirit is broken with sickness or sorrow,
    And comfort is ready to die;
The darkness shall pass, and in gladness tomorrow,
The wounded complete consolation shall borrow
    From his life-giving word, "It is I."

When death is at hand, and the cottage of clay
    Is left with a tremulous sigh,
The gracious forerunner is smoothing the way
For its tenant to pass to unchangeable day,
    Saying, "Be not afraid, it is I."

When the waters are passed, and the glories unknown
    Burst forth on the wondering eye,
The compassionate "Lamb in the midst of the throne"
Shall welcome, encourage, and comfort his own,
    And say, "Be not afraid, it is I."

—NATHANIEL HAWTHORNE

And when a convenient day was come, that Herod on his birthday made a supper to his lords, high captains, and chief estates of Galilee; And when the daughter of the said Herodias came in, and danced, and pleased Herod and them that sat with him, the king said unto the damsel, Ask of me whatsoever thou wilt, and I will give it thee. And he sware unto her, Whatsoever thou shalt ask of me, I will give it thee, unto the half of my kingdom. And she went forth, and said unto her mother, What shall I ask? And she said, The head of John the Baptist.

MARK 6:21–24

Salome

Once on a charger there was laid,
And brought before a royal maid,
As price of attitude and grace,
A guiltless head, a holy face.

It was on Herod's natal day,
Who o'er Judea's land held sway.
He married his own brother's wife,
Wicked Herodias. She the life
Of John the Baptist long had sought,
Because he openly had taught
That she a life unlawful led,
Having her husband's brother wed.

This was he, that saintly John,
Who in the wilderness alone
Abiding, did for clothing wear
A garment made of camel's hair;
Honey and locusts were his food,
And he was most severely good.
He preached penitence and tears,
And waking first the sinner's fears,
Prepared a path, made smooth a way,
For his diviner Master's day.

Herod kept in princely state
His birthday. On his throne he sate,
After the feast, beholding her
Who danced with grace peculiar;
Fair Salome, who did excel
All in that land for dancing well.
The feastful monarch's heart was fired,
And whatsoe'er thing she desired,

Though half his kingdom it should be,
He in his pleasure swore that he
Would give the graceful Salome.
The damsel was Herodias' daughter:
She to the queen hastes, and besought her
To teach her what great gift to name.
Instructed by Herodias, came
The damsel back: to Herod said,
"Give me John the Baptist's head;
And in a charger let it be
Hither straightway brought to me."

Herod her suit would fain deny,
But for his oath's sake must comply.

    When painters would by art express
Beauty in unloveliness,
Thee, Herodias' daughter, thee,
They fittest subject take to be.
They give thy form and features grace;
But ever in thy beauteous face
They show a steadfast cruel gaze,
And eye unpitying; and amaze
In all beholders deep they mark,
That thou betrayest not one spark
Of feeling for the ruthless deed,
That did thy praiseful dance succeed.
For on the head they make you look,
As if a sullen joy you took,
A cruel triumph, wicked pride,
That for your sport a saint has died.

—CHARLES LAMB

When Jesus came into the coasts of Caesarea Philippi, He asked His disciples, saying, Whom do men say that I the Son of man am? And they said, Some say that Thou art John the Baptist: some, Elias; and others, Jeremias, or one of the prophets. He saith unto them, But whom say ye that I am? And Simon Peter answered and said, Thou art the Christ, the Son of the living God.

MATTHEW 16:13—16

104

Son of Man

The doctrine of Jesus consisted in the elevation of the Son of man, that is, in the recognition on the part of man that he, man, was the son of God. In his own individuality Jesus personified the man who has recognized the filial relation with God. He asked his disciples who men said that he was—the Son of man? His disciples replied that some took him for John the Baptist, and some for Elijah. Then came the question, "But who say ye that I am?" And Peter answered, "Thou art the Messiah, the Son of the Living God." Jesus responded, "Flesh and blood hath not revealed it unto thee, but My Father which is in heaven"; meaning that Peter understood, not through faith in human explanations, but because, feeling himself to be the son of God, he understood that Jesus was also the Son of God. And after having explained to Peter that the true faith is founded upon the perception of the final relation to God, Jesus charged his other disciples that they should tell no man that he was the Messiah. After this, Jesus told them that, although he might suffer many things and be put to death, he—that is his doctrine—would be triumphantly re-established.

—LEO TOLSTOY

GOSPEL

*But when He had turned about and looked on His
disciples, He rebuked Peter, saying, Get thee behind
me, Satan: for thou savourest not the things that be
of God, but the things that be of men.*

MARK 8:33

"Retro Me, Sathana"

Get thee behind me. Even as heavy-curled,
    Stooping against the wind, a charioteer
    Is snatched from out his chariot by the hair,
So shall Time be; and as the void car; hurled
Abroad by reinless steeds, even so the world:
    Yea, even as chariot-dust upon the air,
    It shall be sought and not found anywhere.

Get thee behind me, Satan. Oft unfurled,
Thy perilous wings can beat and break like lath
    Much mightiness of me to win thee praise.
    Leave these weak feet to tread in narrow ways.
Thou still, upon the broad vine-sheltered path,
Mayst wait the turning of the phials of wrath
    For certain years, for certain months and days.

—DANTE GABRIEL ROSSETTI

And after six days Jesus taketh Peter, James, and John his brother, and bringeth them up into an high mountain apart, and was transfigured before them: and His face did shine as the sun, and His raiment was white as the light. And, behold, there appeared unto them Moses and Elias talking with Him. Then answered Peter, and said unto Jesus, Lord, it is good for us to be here: if Thou wilt, let us make here three tabernacles; one for Thee, and one for Moses, and one for Elias. While he yet spake, behold, a bright cloud overshadowed them: and behold a voice out of the cloud, which said, This is my beloved Son, in whom I am well pleased; hear ye Him. And when the disciples heard it, they fell on their face, and were sore afraid. And Jesus came and touched them, and said, Arise, and be not afraid. And when they had lifted up their eyes, they saw no man, save Jesus only. And as they came down from the mountain, Jesus charged them, saying, Tell the vision to no man, until the Son of man be risen again from the dead.

Matthew 17:1—9

In the Mountain

JAMES. I have brought our cloaks. . . . Look at the stars. . . . Spread above the earth like a robe of glory.

PETER. But nothing to compare with the glory we saw today in the mountain.

JAMES. No. Tell me, Simon Peter—what did you see? Was it the same for all of us?

PETER. I was tired with the climb. . . . I watched him for a time as he stood and prayed, never speaking, never moving, with his face toward Jerusalem . . . as though he saw nothing but some strange inward vision that held him entranced. . . . I tried to pray too, but no thoughts would come. . . . It seemed to go on for ever. . . .

JOHN. As though time had stopped.

PETER. I think I lost myself a little . . . there in the silence . . . For the next thing I knew was a great terror, as though I was drowning in it—and when I looked at his face, it was not of this earth. It was . . . it was like . . . it is a thing I dare not think of . . .

JAMES. Don't, Peter. We saw it too.

PETER. And his garments whiter than the light—the way no fuller on earth could whiten them. . . . And those two others were with him . . . They spoke together, but I couldn't tell what they said. . . . The glory was upon them both and I knew them for blessed Moses that talked with God in Sinai, and holy Elijah, who passed up to Heaven in light and fire . . . And it seemed that what I saw was the reality, and the earth and the sky only a dream . . . yet I knew all the time that the sun was shining, and I could feel the rough stems of the heather between my fingers.

JAMES. I had lost touch with everything—

except John's hand in mine.

JOHN. Dear James!—I felt you, but as though we were children again—do you remember?—when the great thunderbolt fell, and I was frightened.

JAMES. Oh, John—my little brother, John. It is you now that stand between me and fear.

JOHN. I was afraid too. Peter was the bravest. He spoke.

PETER. Yes—but such nonsense! I thought the vision was departing. I remember calling out: "Lord—it's good to be here. Can't we build three tabernacles for you and Moses and Elijah, and all stay like this for ever?"—so stupid—but I didn't know what I was saying. . . . I thought of the Ark in the wilderness and the glory of the Lord in the pillar of fire . . . all mixed up somehow with the Holy City and the Feast of Tabernacles. . . . And then, and then—the fire and the light were all about us . . . and the Voice . . . was it without us or within? . . . and was it a voice at all?

JOHN. It filled everything—there was nothing in the world but the voice: "This is My beloved Son, hear Him."

JAMES. And after that—nothing. Only the hills and the sky, and Jesus standing there alone.

PETER. He held out his hand, and I was afraid to touch him . . . But he was just the same . . . as though nothing had changed in him.

JOHN. I think the change was not in him but in us. I think we had seen him for a moment as he always is.

—DOROTHY L. SAYERS

Jesus and the Twelve

𝒪ur Lord Jesus and His disciples are turning homeward towards Capharnaum. The twelve are easily tired now; so much has happened on this journey. It is the same every single time they go forth in company with the Master. At each step their poor, weak, human hearts and their slow-thinking brains have had to take in some new impression—bewildering, curious happenings and puzzling words from the Lord's mouth. Let us try to think of all that the Evangelists in their brevity have not described for us.

The long wanderings over the hard Roman roads—they are so tired of walking on a road that it seems almost a rest to strike off for a change on a stony mountain path. And all the time they have been in a multitude of people, surrounded by crowding faces, brown and whitish-yellow roundels, bobbing up and down over the swelling waves of garments, blue, white and brown.

There are faces stirred with emotion, rapt faces, the haggard faces of the sick, faces with ugly-looking sores eating into them. Some gaze with a beseeching, anxious look; others are bound in gloom—mocking, arrogant, sneering, indifferent faces. From them all, dust is whirled towards the sky as they push forward, swaying hither and thither. It is a hot journey in the midst of such a throng; and how they smell—breath tainted with onion; sweaty clothes; the women's cheap, oily scents!

Lively, inquisitive little street-boys elbow themselves forward in the crowd and insist on seeing all that is happening; and they don't spare their shrill voices.

But the twelve apostles are themselves men of the people, and these ways of the people are homely and familiar to them; they mean well when they try to protect Jesus against the women and small boys who press upon Him, and they have more kindly feeling than we give them credit for when we read the Evangelists' account . . .

But since He has chosen them to be His friends, these twelve men seem to have become separated from the mass in a special way. It is around their Lord and Master that all this seething, turbulent sea of people billows up and down. He stands in the middle, all eyes fixed on Him; and together with Him stand these twelve plain, peasant men, facing all the rest; some of these waves as they break throw their spray at them also. Indeed, they have already had some experience of being themselves the centre without Jesus, living and visible, at their side. Were they not sent out two by two to proclaim that the Kingdom of Heaven was at hand, and had they not all been tested in this fight against demons?

And three of these, Peter, James and John, bear in their minds while they now travel towards Capharnaum the memory of the Mount of Transfiguration—in a dazzling and mysterious moment they had seen something of their Lord's true glory. When they came down from the mountain they found themselves right in the middle of the crowd surrounding the mind-sick child and the other disciples who had vainly tried to drive out the unclean spirit from the boy; and again they saw a proof of the Master's power. And while their hearts were overflowing with triumphant gladness about this, Jesus spoke to them dark words of death and resurrection for which they could find no sense.

—SIGRID UNDSET

And if thine eye offend thee, pluck it out, and cast it from thee: it is better for thee to enter into life with one eye, rather than having two eyes to be cast into hell fire.

MATTHEW 18:9

A Shropshire Lad: Poem 45

If it chance your eye offend you,
    Pluck it out, lad, and be sound:
'Twill hurt, but here are salves to friend you,
    And many a balsam grows on ground.

And if your hand or foot offend you,
    Cut it off, lad, and be whole;
But play the man, stand up and end you,
    When your sickness is your soul.

              —A. E. HOUSMAN

After these things the Lord appointed other seventy also, and sent them two and two before His face into every city and place, whither He himself would come. Therefore said He unto them, The harvest truly is great, but the labourers are few: pray ye therefore the Lord of the harvest, that He would send forth labourers into His harvest. Go your ways: behold, I send you forth as lambs among wolves. Carry neither purse, nor scrip, nor shoes: and salute no man by the way.

              LUKE 10:1—4

Salutation

Christ, I have read, did to His chaplains say,
Sending them forth, Salute no man by th'way:
Not that He taught His ministers to be
Unsmooth, or sour, to all civility;
But to instruct them, to avoid all snares

Of tardidation in the Lord's affairs.
Manners are good: but till his errand ends,
Salute we must, nor strangers, kin, or friends.

—Robert Herrick

And, behold, a certain lawyer stood up, and tempted Him, saying, Master, what shall I do to inherit eternal life? He said unto him, What is written in the law? how readest thou? And he answering said, Thou shalt love the Lord thy God with all thy heart, and with all thy soul, and with all thy strength, and with all thy mind; and thy neighbour as thyself. And He said unto him, Thou hast answered right: this do, and thou shalt live. But he, willing to justify himself, said unto Jesus, And who is my neighbour? And Jesus answering said, A certain man went down from Jerusalem to Jericho, and fell among thieves, which stripped him of his raiment, and wounded him, and departed, leaving him half dead. And by chance there came down a certain priest that way: and when he saw him, he passed by on the other side. And likewise a Levite, when he was at the place, came and looked on him, and passed by on the other side. But a certain Samaritan, as he journeyed, came where he was: and when he saw him, he had compassion on him, And went to him, and bound up his wounds, pouring in oil and wine, and set him on his own beast, and brought him to an inn, and took care of him. And on the morrow when he departed,

parted in two; the hands folded and still; and the clothes on him like everyone's. "What sort of Christ is this?" I thought. "Such an ordinary, ordinary man. It cannot be." I turned away, but I had hardly turned my eyes from this ordinary man when I felt again that it was really none other than Christ standing beside me. Suddenly my heart sank and I came to myself. Only then I realized that just such a face is the face of Christ—a face like all men's faces.

—IVAN TURGENEV

But one thing is needful: and Mary hath chosen that good part, which shall not be taken away from her.

LUKE 10:42

I must work the works of Him that sent me, while it is day: the night cometh, when no man can work.

JOHN 9:4

Repent, Resolve

(From *Jane Eyre*. After Jane rejects the marriage proposal of St. John Rivers, he leaves her with this admonition.)

". . . I listen to my duty, and keep steadily in view my first aim—to do all things to the glory of God. My Master was long-suffering: so will I be. I cannot give you up to perdition as a vessel of wrath: repent—resolve; while there is yet time. Remember, we are bid to work while it is day—warned that 'the night cometh when no man shall work.' Remember the fate of Dives, who had his good things in this life. God give you strength to choose that better part which shall not be taken from you!"

—CHARLOTTE BRONTË

Now it came to pass, as they went, that He entered into a certain village: and a certain woman named Martha received Him into her house. And she had a sister called Mary, which also sat at Jesus' feet, and heard His word. But Martha was cumbered about much serving, and came to Him, and said, Lord, dost thou not care that my sister hath left me to serve alone? bid her therefore that she help me. And Jesus answered and said unto her, Martha, Martha, thou art careful and troubled about many

things: But one thing is needful: and Mary hath chosen that good part, which shall not be taken away from her.

LUKE 10:38—42

The Sons of Martha

The Sons of Mary seldom bother, for they have
    inherited that good part;
But the Sons of Martha favour their Mother of the
    careful soul and the troubled heart.
And because she lost her temper once, and because
    she was rude to the Lord her Guest,
Her Sons must wait upon Mary's Sons, world
    without end, reprieve, or rest.

It is their care in all the ages to take the buffet and
    cushion the shock.
It is their care that the gear engages; it is their care
    that the switches lock.
It is their care that the wheels run truly; it is their
    care to embark and entrain,
Tally, transport, and deliver duly the Sons of Mary
    by land and main.

They say to mountains, "Be ye removed." They say
    to the lesser floods, "Be dry."

Under their rods are the rocks reproved—they are
    not afraid of that which is high.
Then do the hill-tops shake to the summit—then is
    the bed of the deep laid bare,
That the Sons of Mary may overcome it, pleasantly
    sleeping and unaware.

They do not preach that their God will rouse them
    a little before the nuts work loose.
They do not teach that His Pity allows them to
    drop their job when they dam'-well choose.
As in the thronged and the lighted ways, so in the
    dark and the desert they stand,
Wary and watchful all their days that their
    brethren's days may be long in the land.

Raise ye the stone or cleave the wood to make a
    path more fair or flat—
Lo, it is black already with blood some Son of
    Martha spilled for that!
Not as a ladder from earth to Heaven, not as a
    witness to any creed,
But simple service simply given to his own kind in
    their common need.

And the Sons of Mary smile and are blessed—they
    know the Angels are on their side.
They know in them is the Grace confessed, and for
    them are the Mercies multiplied.
They sit at the Feet—they hear the Word—they see
    how truly the Promise runs.

They have cast the burden upon the Lord, and—the Lord He lays it on Martha's Sons!

—RUDYARD KIPLING

And as Jesus passed by, He saw a man which was blind from his birth. And His disciples asked Him, saying, Master, who did sin, this man, or his parents, that he was born blind? Jesus answered, Neither hath this man sinned, nor his parents: but that the works of God should be made manifest in him. I must work the works of Him that sent me, while it is day: the night cometh, when no man can work. As long as I am in the world, I am the light of the world. When He had thus spoken, He spat on the ground, and made clay of the spittle, and He anointed the eyes of the blind man with the clay, And said unto him, Go, wash in the pool of Siloam, (which is by interpretation, Sent.) He went his way therefore, and washed, and came seeing.

JOHN 9:1—7

GOSPEL

Receive Thy Sight

When the blind suppliant in the way,
    By friendly hands to Jesus led,
Prayed to behold the light of day,
    "Receive thy sight," the Saviour said.

At once he saw the pleasant rays
    That lit the glorious firmament;
And, with firm step and words of praise,
    He followed where the Master went.

Look down in pity, Lord, we pray,
    On eyes oppressed by moral night,
And touch the darkened lids and say
    The gracious words, "Receive thy sight."

Then, in clear daylight, shall we see
    Where walked the sinless Son of God;
And, aided by new strength from Thee,
    Press onward in the path He trod.

—WILLIAM CULLEN BRYANT

from "On the Death of a Friend's Child"

'Tis sorrow builds the shining ladder up,
Whose golden rounds are our calamities,
Whereon our firm feet planting, nearer God

122

The spirit climbs, and hath its eyes unsealed.
True is it that Death's face seems stern and cold,
When he is sent to summon those we love,
But all God's angels come to us disguised;
Sorrow and sickness, poverty and death,
One after other lift their frowning masks,
And we behold the seraph's face beneath,
All radiant with the glory and the calm
Of having looked upon the front of God.
With every anguish of our earthly part
The spirit's sight grows clearer; this was meant
When Jesus touched the blind man's lids with clay.
Life is the jailer; Death the angel sent
To draw the unwilling bolts and set us free.

—James Russell Lowell

I am the good shepherd, and know my sheep, and am known of mine. As the Father knoweth me, even so know I the Father: and I lay down my life for the sheep.

John 10:14—15

The Good Shepherd

Shepherd! that with thin amorous, sylvan song
Hast broken the slumber which encompassed me,—
That mad'st thy crook from the accursed tree,
On which thy powerful arms were stretched so long!
Lead me to mercy's ever-flowing fountains;
For thou my shepherd, guard, and guide shalt be;
I will obey thy voice, and wait to see
Thy feet all beautiful upon the mountains.
Here, Shepherd!—thou who for thy flock art dying,
O, wash away these scarlet sins, for thou
Rejoicest at the contrite sinner's vow.
O, wait!—to thee my weary soul is crying,—
Wait for me!—Yet why ask it, when I see,
With feet nailed to the cross, thou'rt waiting still
  for me!

—Henry Wadsworth Longfellow

For the Son of man is come to save that which was lost. How think ye? if a man have an hundred sheep, and one of them be gone astray, doth he not leave the ninety and nine, and goeth into the mountains, and seeketh that which is gone astray? And if so be that he find it, verily I say unto you, he rejoiceth more of that sheep, than of the ninety and nine which went not astray. Even so it is not the will of your Father which is in heaven, that one of these little ones should perish.

Matthew 18:11—14

Is One Worth Seeking?

O Shepherd with the bleeding Feet,
Good Shepherd with the pleading Voice,
    What seekest Thou from hill to hill?
Sweet were the valley pastures, sweet
      The sounds of flocks that bleat their joys,
        And eat and drink at will.
Is one worth seeking, when Thou hast of Thine
        Ninety and nine?

—CHRISTINA GEORGINA ROSSETTI

There were present at that season some that told Him of the Galilaeans, whose blood Pilate had mingled with their sacrifices. And Jesus answering said unto them, Suppose ye that these Galilaeans were sinners above all the Galilaeans, because they suffered such things? I tell you, Nay: but, except ye repent, ye shall all likewise perish. Or those eighteen, upon whom the tower in Siloam fell, and slew them, think ye that they were sinners above all men that dwelt in Jerusalem? I tell you, Nay: but, except ye repent, ye shall all likewise perish.

LUKE 13:1—5

The Fallen Tower of Siloam

Should the building totter, run for an archway!
We were there already—already the collapse
Powdered the air with chalk, and shrieking
Of old men crushed under the fallen beams
Dwindled to comic yelps. How not terrible
When the event outran the alarm
And suddenly we were free—

Free to forget how grim it stood,
That tower, and what great fissures ran
Up the west wall, how rotten the under-pinning
At the south-eastern angle. Satire
Had whirled a gentle wind around it,
As if to buttress the worn masonry;
Yet we, waiting, had abstained from satire.

It behoved us, indeed, as poets
To be silent in Siloam, to foretell
No visible calamity. Though kings
Were crowned and gold coin minted still and horses
Still munched at nose-bags in the public sheets,
All such sad emblems were to be condoned:
An old-wives' tale, not ours.

—ROBERT GRAVES

And He said, A certain man had two sons: And the younger of them said to his father, Father, give me the portion of goods that falleth to me. And he divided unto them his living. And not many days after the younger son gathered all together, and took his journey into a far country, and there wasted his substance with riotous living. And when he had spent all, there arose a mighty famine in that land; and he began to be in want. And he went and joined himself to a citizen of that country; and he sent him into his fields to feed swine. And he would fain have filled his belly with the husks that the swine did eat: and no man gave unto him. And when he came to himself, he said, How many hired servants of my father's have bread enough and to spare, and I perish with hunger! I will arise and go to my father, and will say unto him, Father, I have sinned against heaven, and before thee, And am no more worthy to be called thy son: make me as one of thy hired servants. And he arose, and came to his father. But when he was yet a great way off, his father saw him, and had compassion, and ran, and fell on his neck, and kissed him. And the son said unto him, Father, I have sinned against heaven, and in thy sight, and am no more worthy to be called thy son. But the father said to his servants, Bring forth the best robe, and put it on him; and put a ring on his hand, and shoes on his feet: And bring hither the fatted calf, and kill it; and let us eat, and be merry: For this my son was dead, and is alive again; he was lost, and is found.

LUKE 15:11—24

GOSPEL

A Prodigal Son

Does that lamp still burn in my Father's house
　　Which he kindled the night I went away?
I turned once beneath the cedar boughs,
　　And marked it gleam with a golden ray;
　　Did he think to light me home some day?

Hungry here with the crunching swine,
　　Hungry harvest have I to reap;
In a dream I count my Father's kine,
　　I hear the tinkling bells of his sheep,
　　I watch his lambs that browse and leap.

There is plenty of bread at home,
　　His servants have bread enough and to spare;
The purple wine-vat froths with foam,
　　Oil and spices make sweet the air,
　　While I perish hungry and bare.
Rich and blessed those servants, rather
　　Than I who see not my Father's face!
I will arise and go to my Father:—
　　'Fallen from sonship, beggared of grace,
　　Grant me, Father, a servant's place.'

—Christina Georgina Rossetti

*And it came to pass, that the beggar died, and was
carried by the angels into Abraham's bosom: the
rich man also died, and was buried. . .*

Luke 16:22

It Is a Beauteous Evening

It is a beauteous evening, calm and free,
The holy time is quiet as a Nun
Breathless with adoration; the broad sun
Is sinking down in its tranquillity;
The gentleness of heaven broods o'er the Sea:
Listen! the mighty Being is awake,
And doth with his eternal motion make
A sound like thunder—everlastingly.
Dear Child! dear Girl! that walkest with me here,
If thou appear untouched by solemn thought,
Thy nature is not therefore less divine:
Thou liest in Abraham's bosom all the year;
And worship'st at the Temple's inner shrine,
God being with thee when we know it not.

—WILLIAM WORDSWORTH

Jesus wept.

JOHN 11:35

The Two Sayings

Two sayings of the Holy Scriptures beat
Like pulses in the Church's brow and breast;
And by them we find rest in our unrest

And, heart deep in salt-tears, do yet entreat
God's fellowship as if on heavenly seat.
The first is JESUS WEPT,—whereon is prest
Full many a sobbing face that drops its best
And sweetest waters on the record sweet:
And one is where the Christ, denied and scorned,
LOOKED UPON PETER. Oh, to render plain,
By help of having loved a little and mourned,
That look of sovran love and sovran pain
Which HE, who could not sin yet suffered, turned
On him who could reject but not sustain!

—Elizabeth Barrett Browning

Jesus therefore again groaning in Himself cometh to the grave. It was a cave, and a stone lay upon it. Jesus said, Take ye away the stone. Martha, the sister of him that was dead, saith unto Him, Lord, by this time he stinketh: for he hath been dead four days. Jesus saith unto her, Said I not unto thee, that, if thou wouldest believe, thou shouldest see the glory of God? Then they took away the stone from the place where the dead was laid. And Jesus lifted up His eyes, and said, Father, I thank thee that Thou hast heard me. And I knew that Thou hearest Me always: but because of the people which stand by I said it, that they may believe that Thou hast sent Me. And when He thus had spoken, He cried with a loud voice, Lazarus, come forth. And he that was

dead came forth, bound hand and foot with grave-
clothes: and his face was bound about with a nap-
kin. Jesus saith unto them, Loose him, and let him
go.

JOHN 11:38—44

Lazarus

When Lazarus left his charnel-cave,
    And home to Mary's house returned,
    Was this demanded—if he yearned
To hear her weeping by his grave?

"Where wert thou, brother, these four days?"
    There lives no record of reply,
    Which telling what it is to die
Had surely added praise to praise.

From every house the neighbours met,
    The streets were filled with joyful sound
    A solemn gladness even crowned
The purple brows of Olivet.

Behold a man raised up by Christ!
    The rest remaineth unrevealed;
    He told it not; or something sealed
The lips of that Evangelist.

—ALFRED, LORD TENNYSON

The Convert

After one moment when I bowed my head
And the whole world turned over and came upright,
And I came out where the old road shone white,
I walked the ways and heard what all men said,
Forests of tongues, like autumn leaves unshed
Being not unlovable but strange and light;
Old riddles and new creeds, not in despite
But softly, as men smile about the dead.

The sages have a hundred maps to give
That trace their crawling cosmos like a tree,
They rattle reason out through many a sieve
That stores the sand and lets the gold go free:
And all these things are less than dust to me
Because my name is Lazarus and I live.

—G. K. Chesterton

And He spake this parable unto certain which trusted in themselves that they were righteous, and despised others: Two men went up into the temple to pray; the one a Pharisee, and the other a publican. The Pharisee stood and prayed thus with himself, God, I thank thee, that I am not as other men are, extortioners, unjust, adulterers, or even as this publican. I fast twice in the week, I give tithes of all that I possess. And the publican, standing afar off,

would not lift up so much as his eyes unto heaven, but smote upon his breast, saying, God be merciful to me a sinner. I tell you, this man went down to his house justified rather than the other: for every one that exalteth himself shall be abased; and he that humbleth himself shall be exalted.

LUKE 18:9—14

Two Went Up into the Temple to Pray

Two went to pray? o rather say
One went to brag, th'other to pray;

One stands up close and treads on high,
Where th'other dares not send his eye.

One nearer to God's altar trod,
The other to the altar's God.

—RICHARD CRASHAW

And they brought young children to Him, that He should touch them: and His disciples rebuked those that brought them. But when Jesus saw it, He was much displeased, and said unto them, Suffer the little children to come unto Me, and forbid them not:

for of such is the kingdom of God. Verily I say unto you, Whosoever shall not receive the kingdom of God as a little child, he shall not enter therein. And He took them up in His arms, put His hands upon them, and blessed them.

MARK 10:13—16

Little Children

The Disciples asked Him, "Master, who is greatest in the Kingdom of Heaven?" Jesus called a little child to Him, and took him in His arms, and stood among them, and answered, "A child like this. I say unto you that none but those who are as humble as little children shall enter into Heaven. Whosoever shall receive one such little child in my name receiveth me. But whosoever hurts one of them, it were better for him that he had a millstone tied about his neck, and were drowned in the depths of the sea. The Angels are all children." Our Saviour loved the child and loved all children. Yes, and all the world. No one ever loved all people, so well and so truly as He did.

—CHARLES DICKENS

And they came to Jericho: and as He went out of Jericho with His disciples and a great number of people, blind Bartimaeus, the son of Timaeus, sat by the highway side begging. And when he heard that it was Jesus of Nazareth, he began to cry out, and say, Jesus, thou son of David, have mercy on me. And many charged him that he should hold his peace: but he cried the more a great deal, Thou son of David, have mercy on me. And Jesus stood still, and commanded him to be called. And they call the blind man, saying unto him, Be of good comfort, rise; He calleth thee. And he, casting away his garment, rose, and came to Jesus. And Jesus answered and said unto him, What wilt thou that I should do unto thee? The blind man said unto Him, Lord, that I might receive my sight. And Jesus said unto him, Go thy way; thy faith hath made thee whole. And immediately he received his sight, and followed Jesus in the way.

MARK 10:46—52

Blind Bartimeus

Blind Bartimeus at the gates
Of Jericho in darkness waits;
He hears the crowd—he hears a breath
Say, "It is Christ of Nazareth!"
And calls in tones of agony,

"Jesus, have mercy now on me!"
The thronging multitudes increase;
Blind Bartimeus, hold thy peace!
But still, above the noisy crowd,
The beggar's cry is shrill and loud:
Until they say, "He calleth thee!"
"Fear not; arise, He calleth thee!"

Then saith the Christ, as silent stands
The crowd, "What wilt thou at my hands?"
And he replies, "O give me light!
Rabbi, restore the blind man's sight."
And Jesus answers, "Go in peace,
Thy faith from blindness gives release!"

Ye that have eyes yet cannot see,
In darkness and in misery,
Recall those mighty Voices Three,
"Jesus, have mercy now on me!"
"Fear not, arise, and go in peace!
Thy faith from blindness gives release!"

—HENRY WADSWORTH LONGFELLOW

And Jesus entered and passed through Jericho. And, behold, there was a man named Zacchaeus, which was the chief among the publicans, and he was rich. And he sought to see Jesus who He was; and could not for the press, because he was little of

stature. And he ran before, and climbed up into a sycamore tree to see him: for He was to pass that way. And when Jesus came to the place, He looked up, and saw him, and said unto him, Zacchaeus, make haste, and come down; for today I must abide at thy house.

LUKE 19:1—5

Sycamore

Zaccheus he
Did climb the tree
Our Lord to see.

—ROBERT FROST

THE PASSION

And when they drew nigh unto Jerusalem, and were come to Bethphage, unto the mount of Olives, then sent Jesus two disciples, Saying unto them, Go into the village over against you, and straightway ye shall find an ass tied, and a colt with her: loose them, and bring them unto Me. And if any man say aught unto you, ye shall say, The Lord hath need of them, and straightway he will send them. All this was done, that it might be fulfilled which was spoken by the prophet, saying, Tell ye the daughter of Sion, Behold, thy King cometh unto thee, meek, and sitting upon an ass, and a colt the foal of an ass. And the disciples went, and did as Jesus commanded them, And brought the ass, and the colt, and put on them their clothes, and they set Him thereon. And a very great multitude spread their garments in the way; others cut down branches from the trees, and strawed them in the way. And the multitudes that

went before, and that followed, cried, saying,
Hosanna to the son of David: Blessed is He that
cometh in the name of the Lord; Hosanna in the
highest. And when He was come into Jerusalem, all
the city was moved, saying, Who is this? And the
multitude said, This is Jesus the prophet of
Nazareth of Galilee.

MATTHEW 21:1—11

The Donkey

When fisher flew and forests walked
 And figs grew upon thorn,
Some moment when the moon was blood
 Then surely I was born.

With monstrous head and sickening cry
 And ears like errant wings,
The devil's walking parody
 On all four-footed things.

The tattered outlaw of the earth,
 Of ancient crooked will;
Starve, scourge, deride me: I am dumb,
 I keep my secret still.

Fools! For I also had my hour;
 One far fierce hour and sweet:

There was a shout about my ears,
    And palms about my feet.

                    —G. K. CHESTERTON

And when He was come nigh, even now at the descent of the mount of Olives, the whole multitude of the disciples began to rejoice and praise God with a loud voice for all the mighty works that they had seen; Saying, Blessed be the King that cometh in the name of the Lord: peace in heaven, and glory in the highest. And some of the Pharisees from among the multitude said unto Him, Master, rebuke thy disciples. And He answered and said unto them, I tell you that, if these should hold their peace, the stones would immediately cry out.

                    LUKE 19:37—40

The Altar

A broken altar, Lord, thy servant rears,
Made of a heart and cémented with tears;
Whose parts are as thy hand did frame;
No workman's tool hath touched the same.

>   A   heart   alone
>   Is   such   a   stone
>   As   nothing   but
>   Thy power doth cut.
>   Wherefore each part
>   Of my hard heart
>   Meets in this frame
>   To praise thy name;

That if I chance to hold my peace,
These stones to praise thee may not cease.
Oh, let thy blesséd sacrifice be mine,
And sanctify this altar to be thine.

—GEORGE HERBERT

And they come to Jerusalem: and Jesus went into the temple, and began to cast out them that sold and bought in the temple, and overthrew the tables of the moneychangers, and the seats of them that sold doves; And would not suffer that any man should carry any vessel through the temple. And He taught, saying unto them, Is it not written, My house shall be called of all nations the house of prayer? but ye have made it a den of thieves.

MARK 11:15—17

Cleansing of the Temple

*W*hen the Feast was half over Jesus himself came to Jerusalem and went into the Temple. In the porch of the Temple were cattle—cows and bulls—sheep, and cages of pigeons, and money-changers who sat beside counters with money. All this was wanted for the sacrifices to God. But Jesus, entering the Temple and seeing many people there, first of all drove the cattle out of the Temple, and let the pigeons go, and upset the tables of the money-changers, and then said to the people:

"The prophet Isaiah said: 'The house of God is not the Temple in Jerusalem, but the whole world of God's people.' And the prophet Jeremiah also said: 'Do not believe the false saying that this is the house of the Eternal; do not believe it, but change your lives and do not judge falsely, nor oppress the stranger, the widow, and the orphan; do not shed innocent blood, and do not go in the house of God and then say: "Now we can safely do wrong." Make not my house a den of thieves. I, God, rejoice not in your sacrifices, but I rejoice in your love of one another.' Understand that these words of the prophet mean: The living temple is the whole world of people when they love one another. We must serve God not in a Temple, but by living in the spirit and by good actions."

—Leo Tolstoy

GOSPEL

Woe unto you, scribes and Pharisees, hypocrites! for ye are like unto whited sepulchres, which indeed appear beautiful outward, but are within full of dead men's bones, and of all uncleanness. Even so ye also outwardly appear righteous unto men, but within ye are full of hypocrisy and iniquity. Woe unto you, scribes and Pharisees, hypocrites! because ye build the tombs of the prophets, and garnish the sepulchres of the righteous, And say, If we had been in the days of our fathers, we would not have been partakers with them in the blood of the prophets. Wherefore ye be witnesses unto yourselves, that ye are the children of them which killed the prophets. Fill ye up then the measure of your fathers. Ye serpents, ye generation of vipers, how can ye escape the damnation of hell?

MATTHEW 23:27–33

The Place of the Damned

All folks who pretend to religion and grace,
Allow there's a Hell, but dispute of the place;
But if Hell may by logical rules be defined,
The place of the Damned,—I will tell you my mind.
Wherever the Damned do chiefly abound,
Most certainly there is Hell to be found,
Damned Poets, Damned Critics, Damned Block-
Heads, Damned Knaves,

144

THE PASSION

Damned Senators bribed, Damned prostitute Slaves;
Damned Lawyers and Judges, Damned Lords and
    Damned Squires,
Damned Spies and Informers, Damned Friends and
    Damned Liars;
Damned Villains, corrupted in every station,
Damned Time-Serving Priests all over the nation;
And into the bargain, I'll readily give you,
Damned Ignorant Prelates, and Councillors Privy.
Then let us no longer by parsons be flammed,
For we know by these marks, the place of the
    Damned;
And Hell to be sure is at Paris or Rome,
How happy for us, that it is not at home.

—JONATHAN SWIFT

*And He looked up, and saw the rich men casting
their gifts into the treasury. And He saw also a certain poor widow casting in thither two mites. And
He said, Of a truth I say unto you, That this poor
widow hath cast in more than they all: For all these
have of their abundance cast in unto the offerings of
God: but she of her Penury hath cast in all the living
that she had.*

LUKE 21:1—4

The Widow's Mites

*A*s He was teaching them thus, He sat near the public treasury, where people, as they passed along the street, were accustomed to drop money into a box for the poor; and many rich persons, passing while Jesus sat there, had put in a great deal of money. At last there came a poor widow who dropped in two mites, each half a farthing in value, and then went quietly away. Jesus, seeing her do this, as He rose to leave the place called His Disciples about Him, and said to them that that poor widow had been more truly charitable than all the rest who had given money that day; for the others were rich and would never miss what they had given, but she was very poor, and had given those two mites which might have bought her bread to eat.

Let us never forget what the poor widow did, when we think we are charitable.

—CHARLES DICKENS

Then shall the kingdom of heaven be likened unto ten virgins, which took their lamps, and went forth to meet the bridegroom. And five of them were wise, and five were foolish. They that were foolish took their lamps, and took no oil with them: But the wise took oil in their vessels with their lamps. While the bridegroom tarried, they all slumbered

*and slept. And at midnight there was a cry made,
Behold, the bridegroom cometh; go ye out to meet
him. Then all those virgins arose, and trimmed
their lamps. And the foolish said unto the wise,
Give us of your oil; for our lamps are gone out. But
the wise answered, saying, Not so; lest there be not
enough for us and you: but go ye rather to them
that sell, and buy for yourselves. And while they
went to buy, the bridegroom came; and they that
were ready went in with him to the marriage: and
the door was shut. Afterward came also the other
virgins, saying, Lord, Lord, open to us. But he
answered and said, Verily I say unto you, I know
you not. Watch therefore, for ye know neither the
day nor the hour wherein the Son of man cometh.*

MATTHEW 25:1—13

The Dawning

Ah! what time wilt Thou come? When shall that cry
"The Bridegroom's coming!" fill the sky?
Shall it in the evening run
When our words and works are done?
Or will Thy all-surprising light
    Break at midnight,
When either sleep, or some dark pleasure
Possesseth mad man without measure?
Or shall these early, fragrant hours

Gospel

Unlock Thy bowers?
And with their blush of light descry
Thy locks crown'd with eternity?

O at what time soever Thou,
Unknown to us, the heavens wilt bow,
And with Thy angels in the van,
Descend to judge poor careless man,
Grant I may not like puddle lie
In a corrupt security,
Where, if a traveller water crave,
He finds it dead, and in a grave;
But at this restless, vocal spring
All day and night doth run and sing,
And though here born, yet is acquainted
Elsewhere, and flowing keeps untainted;
So let me all my busy age
In Thy free services engage;
And though—while here—of course I must
Have commerce sometimes with poor dust,
And in my flesh, though vile and low,
As this doth in her channel flow,
Yet let my course, my aim, my love,
And chief acquaintance be above;
So when that day and hour shall come,
In which Thy Self will be the sun,
Thou'lt find me dress'd and on my way,
Watching the break of Thy great day.

—Henry Vaughan

Advent Sunday

Behold, the Bridegroom cometh: go ye out
With lighted lamps and garlands round about
To meet Him in a rapture with a shout.

It may be at the midnight, black as pitch,
Earth shalt cast up her poor, cast up her rich.

It may be at the crowing of the cock
Earth shall upheave her depth, uproot her rock.

For lo, the Bridegroom fetcheth home the Bride:
His Hands are Hands she knows, she knows His Side.

Like pure Rebekah at the appointed place,
Veiled, she unveils her face to meet His Face.

Like great Queen Esther in her triumphing,
She triumphs in the Presence of her King.

His Eyes are as a Dove's, and she's Dove-eyed;
He knows His lovely mirror, sister, Bride.

He speaks with Dove-voice of exceeding love,
And she with love-voice of an answering Dove.

Behold, the Bridegroom cometh: go we out
With lamps ablaze and garlands round about
To meet Him in a rapture with a shout.

—Christina Georgina Rossetti

For the Son of Man is as a man taking a far jour-
ney, who left his house, and gave authority to his
servants, and to every man his work, and com-
manded the porter to watch. Watch ye therefore:
for ye know not when the master of the house
cometh, at even, or at midnight or at the cock-
crowing, or in the morning: Lest coming suddenly
he find you sleeping. And what I say unto you I say
unto all, Watch.

MARK 13:34—37

The Lamp

'Tis dead night round about: Horror doth creep
And move on with the shades; stars nod, and sleep,
And through the dark air spin a fiery thread
Such as doth gild the lazy glow-worm's bed.
Yet, burnst thou here, a full day; while I spend
My rest in cares, and to the dark world lend
These flames, as thou dost thine to me, I watch
That hour, which must thy life, and mine dispatch;
But still thou dost out-go me, I can see
Met in thy flames, all acts of piety;
Thy light, is charity; thy heat, is zeal;
And thy aspiring, active fires reveal
Devotion still on wing; Then, thou dost weep
Still as thou burnst, and the warm droppings creep
To measure out thy length, as if thou'dst know

What stock, and how much time were left thee now;
Nor dost thou spend one tear in vain, for still
As thou dissolvst to them, and they distill,
They're stored up in the socket, where they lie,
When all is spent, thy last, and sure supply,
And such is true repentance, every breath
We spend in sighs, is treasure after death;
Only, one point escapes thee; That thy oil
Is still out with thy flame, and so both fail;
But whensoe'er I'm out, both shall be in,
And where thou mad'st an end, there I'll begin.

—HENRY VAUGHAN

*For the kingdom of heaven is as a man travelling into
a far country, who called his own servants, and delivered unto them his goods. And unto one he gave five
talents, to another two, and to another one; to every
man according to his several ability; and straightway
took his journey. Then he that had received the five
talents went and traded with the same, and made
them other five talents. And likewise he that had
received two, he also gained other two. But he that
had received one went and digged in the earth, and
hid his lord's money. After a long time the lord of
those servants cometh, and reckoneth with them.
And so he that had received five talents came and
brought other five talents, saying, Lord, thou deliveredst unto me five talents: behold, I have gained*

beside them five talents more. His lord said unto him, Well done, thou good and faithful servant: thou hast been faithful over a few things, I will make thee ruler over many things: enter thou into the joy of thy lord. He also that had received two talents came and said, Lord, thou deliveredst unto me two talents: behold, I have gained two other talents beside them. His lord said unto him, Well done, good and faithful servant; thou hast been faithful over a few things, I will make thee ruler over many things: enter thou into the joy of thy lord. Then he which had received the one talent came and said, Lord, I knew thee that thou art an hard man, reaping where thou hast not sown, and gathering where thou hast not strawed: And I was afraid, and went and hid thy talent in the earth: lo, there thou hast that is thine. His lord answered and said unto him, Thou wicked and slothful servant, thou knewest that I reap where I sowed not, and gather where I have not strawed.

MATTHEW 25:14—26

When I Consider

When I consider how my light is spent,
    Ere half my days, in this dark world and wide,
    And that one talent which is death to hide
    Lodged with me useless, though my soul more bent
To serve therewith my Maker, and present
    My true account, lest he returning chide,

"Doth God exact day-labour, light denied?"
I fondly ask. But Patience, to prevent
That murmur, soon replies: "God doth not need
    Either man's work or his own gifts; who best
    Bear his mild yoke, they serve him best. His state
Is kingly: thousands at his bidding speed,
    And post o'er land and ocean without rest;
    They also serve who only stand and wait."

—JOHN MILTON

He riseth from supper, and laid aside His garments; and took a towel, and girded Himself. After that He poureth water into a basin, and began to wash the disciples' feet, and to wipe them with the towel wherewith He was girded. Then cometh He to Simon Peter: and Peter saith unto Him, Lord, dost thou wash my feet? Jesus answered and said unto him, What I do thou knowest not now; but thou shalt know hereafter. Peter saith unto Him, Thou shalt never wash my feet. Jesus answered him, If I wash thee not, thou hast no part with Me. Simon Peter saith unto Him, Lord, not my feet only, but also my hands and my head.

JOHN 13:4—8

153

GOSPEL

St. Peter

St. Peter once: "Lord, dost thou wash my feet?"—
    Much more I say: Lord dost thou stand and knock
    At my closed heart more rugged than a rock,
Bolted and barred, for thy soft touch unmeet,
Nor garnished nor in any wise made sweet?
    Owls roost within and dancing satyrs mock.
    Lord, I have heard the crowing of the cock
And have not wept: ah, Lord, thou knowest it.
Yet still I hear thee knocking, still I hear:
    "Open to me, look on me eye to eye,
That I may wring thy heart and make it whole;
And teach thee love because I hold thee dear
    And sup with thee in gladness soul with soul,
    And sup with thee in glory by and by."

—CHRISTINA GEORGINA ROSSETTI

And as they sat and did eat, Jesus said, Verily I say unto you, One of you which eateth with Me shall betray Me. And they began to be sorrowful, and to say unto Him one by one, Is it I? and another said, Is it I? And He answered and said unto them, It is one of the twelve, that dippeth with me in the dish. The Son of man indeed goeth, as it is written of Him: but woe to that man by whom the Son of man is betrayed! good were it for that man if he had never been born.

MARK 14:18—21

Judas Iscariot

The eyes of twenty centuries
Pursue me along corridors to where
I am painted at their ends on many walls.
    Ever-revolving futures recognize
This red hair and red beard, where I am seated
Within the dark cave of the feast of light.
    Out of my heart-shaped shadow I stretch my hand
Across the white table into the dish
But not to dip the bread. It is as though
The cloth on each side of one dove-bright face
Spread dazzling wings on which the apostles ride
Uplifting them into the vision
Where their eyes watch themselves enthroned
    My russet hand across the dish
Plucks enviously against one feather
    But still the rushing wings spurn me below!

    Saint Sebastian of wickedness
I stand: all eyes legitimate arrows piercing through
The darkness of my wickedness. They recognize
My halo hammered from thirty silver pieces
And the hemp rope around my neck
Soft as that spirit's hanging arms
When on my cheek he answered with the kiss
Which cuts for ever—
    My strange stigmata,
All love and hate, all fire and ice!

    But who betrayed whom? O you,

GOSPEL

Whose light gaze forms the azure corridor
Through which those other pouring eyes
Arrow into me—answer! Who
Betrayed whom? Who had foreseen
All, from the first? Who read
In his mind's light from the first day
That the kingdom of heaven on earth must always
Reiterate the garden of Eden,
And each day's revolution be betrayed
Within man's heart each day?

    Who wrapped
The whispering serpent round the tree
And hung between the leaves the glittering purse
And trapped the fangs with God-appointed poison?
    Who knew
I must betray the truth, and made the lie
Betray its truth in me?

    Those hypocrite eyes which aimed at you
Now aim at me. And yet, beyond this world
We are alone, eternal opposites,
Each turning on his pole of truth, your pole
Invisible light, and mine
Becoming what man is. We stare
Across two thousand years, and heaven, and hell,
Into each other's gaze.

—STEPHEN SPENDER

The Last Supper

They are gathered, astounded and disturbed,
round him who, like a sage resolved to his end,
takes himself away from those he belonged to,
and who alien past them flows.
The old loneliness comes over him
that reared him to the doing of his deep acts;
now again will he wander through the olive grove,
and those who love him will take flight before him.

He has summoned them to the last supper
and (as a shot scatters birds out of the sheaves)
he scatters their hands from among the loaves
with his word: they fly across to him;
they flutter anxious through the table's round
and try to find a way out. But he
is everywhere like a twilight-hour.

—RAINER MARIA RILKE

And as they were eating, Jesus took bread, and blessed it, and brake it, and gave it to the disciples, and said, Take, eat; this is My body.

MATTHEW 26:26

This Bread I Break

This bread I break was once the oat,
This wine upon a foreign tree
Plunged in its fruit;
Man in the day or wind at night
Laid the crops low, broke the grape's joy.

Once in this wine the summer blood
Knocked in the flesh that decked the vine,
Once in this bread
The oat was merry in the wind;
Man broke the sun, pulled the wind down.

This flesh you break, this blood you let
Make desolation in the vein,
Were oat and grape
Born of the sensual root and sap;
My wine you drink, my bread you snap.

—DYLAN THOMAS

In My Father's house are many mansions: if it were not so, I would have told you. I go to prepare a place for you.

JOHN 14:2

Mansions

"Houses"—so the Wise Men tell me—
"Mansions"! Mansions must be warm!
Mansions cannot let the tears in,
Mansions must exclude the storm!

"Many Mansions", by "his Father",
I don't know him; snugly built!
Could the Children find the way there—
Some would even trudge tonight!

—EMILY DICKINSON

Jesus saith unto him, I am the way, the truth, and the life: no man cometh unto the Father, but by Me.

JOHN 14:6

He Is the Way

He is the Way.
Follow Him through the Land of Unlikeness;
You will see rare beasts, and have unique
    adventures.

GOSPEL

He is the Truth.
Seek Him in the Kingdom of Anxiety;
You will come to a great city that has
    expected your return for years.

He is the Life.
Love Him in the World of the Flesh;
And at your marriage all its occasions
    shall dance for joy.

—W. H. AUDEN

And they came to a place which was named Gethsemane: and He saith to His disciples, Sit ye here, while I shall pray. And He taketh with Him Peter and James and John, and began to be sore amazed, and to be very heavy; And saith unto them, My soul is exceeding sorrowful unto death: tarry ye here, and watch. And He went forward a little, and fell on the ground, and prayed that, if it were possible, the hour might pass from Him. And He said, Abba, Father, all things are possible unto thee; take away this cup from Me: nevertheless not what I will, but what Thou wilt. And He cometh, and findeth them sleeping, and saith unto Peter, Simon, sleepest thou? couldest not thou watch one hour? Watch ye and pray, lest ye enter into temptation. The spirit truly is ready, but the flesh is weak. And again He went away, and prayed, and spake

the same words. And when He returned, He found them asleep again, (for their eyes were heavy,) neither wist they what to answer Him. And He cometh the third time, and saith unto them, Sleep on now, and take your rest: it is enough, the hour is come; behold, the Son of man is betrayed into the hands of sinners. Rise up, let us go; lo, he that betrayeth Me is at hand. And immediately, while He yet spake, cometh Judas, one of the twelve, and with him a great multitude with swords and staves, from the chief priests and the scribes and the elders. And he that betrayed Him had given them a token, saying, Whomsoever I shall kiss, that same is He; take Him, and lead Him away safely. And as soon as he was come, he goeth straightway to Him, and saith, Master, master; and kissed Him.

MARK 14:32—45

One Hour

*M*ake this present day that [namely, Christ's last] day in thy devotion, and consider what he did, and remember what you have done . . . After the Sacrament he spent the time till night in prayer, in preaching, in Psalms . . . At night he went into the garden to pray, and he spent much time in prayer, how much? Because it is literally expressed, that he prayed there several times, and that returning to his

Disciples after his first prayer, and finding them asleep said, could ye not watch with me one hour, it is collected that he spent three hours in prayer. I dare scarce ask thee whither thou went, or how thou disposed of thyself, when it grew dark and after last night: If that time were spent in a holy recommendation of thy self to God, and a submission of thy will to his, it was spent in a conformity to him. In that time and in those prayers was his agony and bloody sweat. I will hope that thou did pray; but not every ordinary and customary prayer, but prayer actually accompanied with shedding of tears, and dispositively in a readiness to shed blood for his glory in necessary cases, puts thee into a conformity with him.

—JOHN DONNE

The Mystery of Jesus

*J*esus suffers in His passions the torments which men inflict upon Him; but in His agony He suffers the torments which He inflicts on Himself; *turbare semetipsum* (to disturb oneself). This is a suffering from no human, but an almighty hand, for He must be almighty to bear it.

Jesus seeks some comfort at least in His three dearest friends, and they are asleep. He prays them to bear with Him for a little, and they leave Him

with entire indifference, having so little compassion
that it could not prevent their sleeping even for a
moment. And thus Jesus was left alone to the wrath
of God.

Jesus is alone on the earth, without anyone not
only to feel and share His suffering, but even to
know of it; He and Heaven were alone in that
knowledge.

Jesus is in a garden, not of delight as the first
Adam, where he lost himself and the whole human
race, but in one of agony, where He saved Himself
and the whole human race.

—BLAISE PASCAL

Garden of Gethsemane

The turn in the road was illumined
By the indiffered glimmer of the remote stars.
The road led around the Mount of Olives;
Below, in its valley, the Brook Kedron ran.

Halfway, the small meadow dipped in a sharp break;
Beyond it began the great Milky Way,
While the silver-gray olives still strained forward
As if to stride onward upon empty air.

Furthest away was someone's garden plot.
He left His disciples outside the stone fence

Saying, "My soul is exceeding sorrowful, even unto
    death;
Tarry ye here, and watch with me."

He had rejected without resistance
Dominion over all things and the power to work
    miracles,
As though these had been His only on loan
And now was as all mortals are, even as we.

Night's distance seemed the very brink
Of annihilation, of nonexistence.
The universe's span was void of any life;
The garden only was a coign of being.

And peering into these black abysses—
Void, without end and without beginning
His brow sweating blood, He pleaded with His Father
That this cup of death might pass from Him.

Having eased His mortal anguish through prayer,
He left the garden. Beyond its wall His disciples,
Overcome with sleep, sprawled on the ground
In the wayside feathergrass.

He awakened them: "God hath granted you to live
During my days on earth, and yet you lie there
    sprawling.
Behold, the hour is at hand, and the Son of Man
Shall betray Himself into the hands of sinners."

He had scarcely spoken when, coming from none
    knew where,
A throng of slaves sprang up, a host of vagrant men
With swords and torches, and at their head stood
    Judas
With the perfidious kiss writhing on his lips.

                        —BORIS PASTERNAK

The Garden of Olives

He went up under the gray foliage
all gray and merging with the olive lands
and laid his forehead that was full of dust
deep in the dustiness of his hot hands.

After everything this. And this was the end.
Now I must go, while I am turning blind,
and why dost Thou so will, that I must say
Thou art, when I myself do no more find Thee.

I find Thee no more. Not within me, no.
Not in the others. Not within this rock.
I find thee no more. I am alone.

I am alone with all mankind's grief,
which I through Thee to lighten undertook,
Thou who art not. O nameless shame. . . .

GOSPEL

Later it was said: an angel came.

Why an angel? Alas it was the night
leafing indifferently among the trees.
The disciples stirred in their dreams.
Why an angel? Alas it was the night.

The night that came was no uncommon night;
hundred like it go by.
Then dogs sleep, and then stones lie.
Alas a sad night, alas any night
that waits till it be morning again.

For angels come not to such suppliants,
and nights do not round about such grow large.
Who lose themselves by all things are let go,
and they are abandoned of their fathers
and shut out of their mothers' hearts.

—RAINER MARIA RILKE

*And the Lord turned, and looked upon Peter. And
Peter remembered the word of the Lord, how He
had said unto him, Before the cock crow, thou shalt
deny Me thrice. And Peter went out, and wept bit-
terly.*

LUKE 22:61—62

The Lord Turned, and Looked upon Peter

The Saviour looked on Peter. Ay, no word,
    No gesture of reproach! the heavens serene,
    Though heavy with armed justice, did not lean
Their thunders that way! the forsaken Lord
Looked only on the traitor. None record
    What that look was, none guess: for those who
        have seen
    Wronged lovers loving through a death-pang
        keen,
Or pale-cheeked martyrs smiling to a sword,
Have missed Jehovah at the judgment-call.
    And Peter, from the height of blasphemy—
"I never knew this man"—did quail and fall,
    As knowing straight that God—and turned free
And went out speechless from the face of all,
    And filled the silence, weeping bitterly.

—Elizabeth Barrett Browning

Then Pilate therefore took Jesus, and scourged Him. And the soldiers plaited a crown of thorns, and put it on His head, and they put on Him a purple robe, And said, Hail, King of the Jews! and they smote Him with their hands. Pilate therefore went forth again, and saith unto them, Behold, I bring Him forth to you, that ye may know that I find no

fault in Him. Then came Jesus forth, wearing the crown of thorns, and the purple robe. And Pilate saith unto them, Behold the Man!

JOHN 19:1—5

A Grief Like Mine

Ah, how they scourge Me! Yet My tenderness
Doubles each lash: and yet their bitterness
Winds up My grief to a mysteriousness:
    Was ever grief like Mine?

And now I am deliver'd unto death;
Which each one calls for so with utmost breath,
That he before Me well-nigh suffereth:
    Was ever grief like Mine?

The soldiers lead Me to the common hall:
There they deride Me, they abuse Me all;
Yet for twelve Heav'nly legions I could call:
    Was ever grief like Mine?

Then with a scarlet robe they Me array,
Which shows My blood to be the only way
And cordial left to repair man's decay:
    Was ever grief like Mine?

—GEORGE HERBERT

THE PASSION

And when they had plaited a crown of thorns, they put it upon His head, and a reed in His right hand: and they bowed the knee before Him, and mocked Him, saying, Hail, King of the Jews!

MATTHEW 27:29

One Crown That No One Seeks

One crown that no one seeks
And yet the highest head
Its isolation coveted
Its stigma deified

While Pontius Pilate lives
In whatsoever hell
That coronation pierces him
He recollects it well

—EMILY DICKINSON

The Coronet

When with the thorns with which I long, too long,
    With many a piercing wound,
    My Saviour's head have crowned,
I seek with garlands to redress that wrong—

GOSPEL

Through every garden, every mead,
I gather flowers (my fruits are only flowers)
 Dismantling all the fragrant towers
That once adorned my shepherdess's head:
And now, when I have summed up all my store,
 Thinking (so I myself deceive)
 So rich a chaplet thence to weave
As never yet the King of Glory wore,
 Alas! I find the Serpent old,
 Twining in his speckled breast,
 About the flowers disguised does fold,
 With wreaths of fame and interest.
Ah foolish man, that would'st debase with them,
And mortal glory, Heaven's diadem!
But thou who only could'st the Serpent tame,
Either his slippery knots at once untie,
And disentangle all his winding snare,
Or shatter too with him my curious frame,
And let these wither so that he may die,
Though set with skill, and chosen out with care,
That they, while thou on both their spoils dost read,
May crown thy feet, that could not crown thy head.

—ANDREW MARVELL

And Pilate asked Him, Art Thou the King of the Jews? And He answering said unto them, Thou sayest it. And the chief priests accused Him of many things: but He answered nothing.

MARK 15:2—3

And He Answered Them Nothing

O Mighty *Nothing*! unto thee,
Nothing, we owe all things that be.
God spake once when he all things made,
He saved all when he *Nothing* said.
The world was made of *Nothing* then;
'Tis made by *Nothing* now again.

—RICHARD CRASHAW

THE CRUCIFIXION

And when they were come to the place, which is called Calvary, there they crucified Him, and the malefactors, one on the right hand, and the other on the left.

LUKE 23:33

This Cross-Tree Here

This Cross-Tree here
Doth   Jesus   bear.
Who sweetened first,
The Death accursed.
Here all things ready are, make haste, make haste away;
For, long this work will be, and very short this day.
Why then, go on to act: Here's wonders to be done,
Before the last least sand of thy ninth hour be run;
Or ere dark clouds do dull, or dead the mid-day's sun.
Act when thou wilt,
Blood will be spilt;
Pure balm, that shall
Bring health to all.
Why then, begin
To pour first in
Some drops of wine,
In stead of brine,
To search the wound,
So long unsound:
And, when that's done,
Let oil, next, run,
To cure the sore
Sin made before.
And O! Dear Christ,
E'en as thou di'st,
Look down, and see
Us weep for Thee.
And tho' (Love knows)
Thy dreadful woes
We   cannot   ease;
Yet do thou please,
Who   mercy   art,
T'accept each heart,
That gladly would
Help, if it could.
Mean while, let me,
Beneath this Tree,
This honor have
To make my grave.

—ROBERT HERRICK

Crucify Him

That you may know what the people meant when they said, "Crucify Him!" I must tell you that in those times, which were very cruel times indeed (let us thank God and Jesus Christ that they are past!) it was the custom to kill people who were sentenced to death, by nailing them alive on a great wooden cross, planted upright in the ground, and leaving them there, exposed to the sun and wind, and day and night, until they died of pain and thirst. It was the custom too, to make them walk to the place of execution, carrying the cross-piece of wood to which their hands were to be afterwards nailed, that their shame and suffering might be the greater.

Bearing His cross upon His shoulder, like the commonest and most wicked criminal, Our Blessed Saviour, Jesus Christ, surrounded by the persecuting crowd, went out of Jerusalem to a place called, in the Hebrew language, *Golgotha*; that is, the place of a skull. And being come to a hill called Mount Calvary, they hammered cruel nails through His hands and feet, and nailed Him on the cross, between two other crosses, on each of which a common thief was nailed in agony. Over His head they fastened this writing: "Jesus of Nazareth, the King of the Jews"—in three languages: in Hebrew, in Greek, and in Latin.

Meantime, a guard of four soldiers, sitting on the ground, divided His clothes (which they had taken off) into four parcels for themselves, and cast lots for His coat, and sat there, gambling and talking, while He suffered. They offered Him vinegar to drink, mixed with gall; and wine, mixed with myrrh; but He took none. And the wicked people who passed that way mocked Him, and said, "If Thou be the Son of God, come down from the cross." The chief priests also mocked Him, and said, "He came to save sinners. Let Him save Himself!" One of the thieves, too, railed at Him, in his torture, and said, "If Thou be Christ, save Thyself, and us." But the other thief, who was penitent, said, "Lord! Remember me when Thou comest into Thy Kingdom!" And Jesus answered, "To-day thou shalt be with me in Paradise."

—CHARLES DICKENS

The Legend of the Crossbill

On the cross of the dying Saviour
　　Heavenward lifts his eyelids calm,
Feels, but scarcely feels, a trembling
　　In his pierced and bleeding palm.

And by all the world forsaken,
　　Sees he how with zealous care
At the ruthless nail of iron
　　A little bird is striving there.

Stained with blood and never tiring,
 With its beak it doth not cease,
From the cross 'twould free the Saviour,
 Its Creator's Son release.

And the Saviour speaks in mildness:
 "Blest be thou of all the good!
Bear, as token of this moment,
 Marks of blood and holy rood!"

And that bird is called the crossbill;
 Covered all with blood so clear,
In the groves of pine it singeth
 Songs, like legends, strange to hear.

—HENRY WADSWORTH LONGFELLOW

Tortoise Shell

The Cross, the Cross
Goes deeper in than we know,
Deeper into life;
Right into the marrow
And through the bone.

Along the back of the baby tortoise
The scales are locked in an arch like a bridge,
Scale-lapping, like a lobster's sections
Or a bee's.

Then crossways down his sides
Tiger-stripes and wasp-bands.

Five, and five again, and five again,
And round the edges twenty-five little ones,
The sections of the baby tortoise shell.
Four, and a keystone;
Four, and a keystone;
Four, and a keystone;
Then twenty-four, and a tiny little keystone.

It needed Pythagoras to see life playing with counters
    on the living back
Of the baby tortoise;
Life establishing the first eternal mathematical tablet,
Not in stone, like the Judean Lord, or bronze, but in
    life-clouded, life-rosy tortoise shell.
The first little mathematical gentleman
Stepping, wee mite, in his loose trousers
Under all the eternal dome of mathematical law.

Fives, and tens,
Threes and fours and twelves,
All the *volte-face* of decimals,
The whirligig of dozens and the pinnacle of seven.

Turn him on his back,
The kicking little beetle,
And there again, on his shell-tender, earth-touching
    belly,
The long cleavage of division, upright of the eternal
    cross

And on either side count five,
On each side, two above, on each side, two below
The dark bar horizontal.

The Cross!
It goes right through him, the sprottling insect,
Through his cross-wise cloven psyche,
Through his five-fold complex-nature.

So turn him over on his toes again;
Four pin-point toes, and a problematical thumb-piece,
Four rowing limbs, and one wedge-balancing head,
Four and one makes five, which is the clue to all
     mathematics.

The Lord wrote it all down on the little slate
Of the baby tortoise.
Outward and visible indication of the plan within,
The complex, manifold involvedness of an individual
     creature
Plotted out
On this small bird, this pediment
Of all creation,
This slow one.

—D. H. LAWRENCE

And they bring Him unto the place Golgotha, which is, being interpreted, The place of a skull. And they gave Him to drink wine mingled with myrrh: but He received it not. And when they had crucified him, they parted His garments, casting lots upon them, what every man should take. And it was the third hour, and they crucified Him. And the superscription of His accusation was written over, THE KING OF THE JEWS. And with him they crucify two thieves; the one on His right hand, and the other on His left.

MARK 15:22—27

Still Falls the Rain
(*The Raids, 1940, night and dawn*)

Still falls the Rain—
Dark as the world of man, black as our loss—
Blind as the nineteen hundred and forty nails
Upon the Cross.

Still falls the Rain
With a sound like the pulse of the heart that is
    changed to the hammer-beat
In the Potter's Field, and the sound of the impious feet

On the tomb:
    Still falls the Rain

CRUCIFIXION

In the Field of Blood where the small hopes breed
    and the human brain
Nurtures its greed, that worm with the brow of Cain.

Still falls the Rain
At the feet of the Starved Man hung upon the Cross.
Christ that each day, each night, nails there,
                have mercy on us—
On Dives and on Lazarus:
Under the Rain the sore and the gold are as one.

Still falls the Rain—
Still falls the Blood from the Starved Man's wounded
    Side:
He bears in his Heart all wounds,—those of the
                light that died,
The last faint spark
In the self-murdered heart, the wounds of the sad
                uncomprehending dark,
The wounds of the baited bear,—
The blind and weeping bear whom the keepers beat
On his helpless flesh . . . the tears of the hunted hare.

Still falls the Rain—
Then—O Ile leape up to my God: who pulls me
    doune—
See, see where Christ's blood streames in the
    firmament:
It flows from the Brow we nailed upon the tree
Deep to the dying, to the thirsting heart
That holds the fires of the world,—dark-smirched

with pain
As Caesar's laurel crown.

Then sounds the voice of One who like the heart of
man
Was once a child who among beasts has lain—
"Still do I love, still shed my innocent light, my
Blood, for thee."

—EDITH SITWELL

*And, behold, the veil of the temple was rent in twain
from the top to the bottom; and the earth did quake,
and the rocks rent; And the graves were opened; and
many bodies of the saints which slept arose, And
came out of the graves after His resurrection, and
went into the holy city, and appeared unto many.
Now when the centurion, and they that were with
Him, watching Jesus, saw the earthquake, and those
things that were done, they feared greatly, saying,
Truly this was the Son of God.*

MATTHEW 27:51—54

The Crucifixion

Sunlight upon Judaea's hills!
    And on the waves of Galilee,—
On Jordan's stream, and on the rills
    That feed the dead and sleeping sea!
Most freshly from the green wood springs
The light breeze on its scented wings;
And gayly quiver in the sun
The cedar tops of Lebanon!

A few more hours,—a change hath come!
    The sky is dark without a cloud!
The shouts of wrath and joy are dumb,
    And proud knees unto earth are bowed.
A change is on the hill of Death,
The helmed watchers pant for breath,
And turn with wild and maniac eyes
From the dark scene of sacrifice!

That Sacrifice!—the death of Him,—
    The High and ever Holy One!
Well may the conscious Heaven grow dim,
    And blacken the beholding Sun.
The wonted light hath fled away,
Night settles on the middle day,
And earthquake from his caverned bed
Is waking with a thrill of dread!

The dead are waking underneath!
    Their prison door is rent away!

GOSPEL

And, ghastly with the seal of death,
　　They wander in the eye of day!
The temple of the Cherubim,
The House of God is cold and dim;
A curse is on its trembling walls,
Its mighty veil asunder falls!

Well may the cavern-depths of Earth
　　Be shaken, and her mountains nod;
Well may the sheeted dead come forth
　　To gaze upon a suffering God!
Well may the temple-shrine grow dim,
And shadows veil the Cherubim,
When He, the chosen one of Heaven,
A sacrifice for guilt is given!

And shall the sinful heart, alone,
　　Behold unmoved the atoning hour,
When Nature trembles on her throne,
　　And Death resigns his iron power?
O, shall the heart—whose sinfulness
Gave keenness to his sore distress,
And added to his tears of blood—
Refuse its trembling gratitude!

—JOHN GREENLEAF WHITTIER

*And when the sixth hour was come, there was
darkness over the whole land until the ninth hour.*

MARK 15:33

CRUCIFIXION

I Bore with Thee, Long, Weary Days

I bore with thee, long, weary days and nights,
  Through many pangs of heart, through many
    tears;
I bore with thee, thy hardness, coldness, slights,
  For three and thirty years.

Who else had dared for thee what I have dared?
  I plunged the depth most deep from bliss above;
I not My flesh, I not My spirit spared:
  Give thou Me love for love.

For thee I thirsted in the daily drouth,
  For thee I trembled in the nightly frost:
Much sweeter thou than honey to My mouth;
  Why wilt thou still be lost?

I bore thee on My shoulders, and rejoiced:
  Men only marked upon My shoulders borne
The branding cross; and shouted hungry-voiced,
  Or wagged their heads in scorn.

Thee did nails grave upon My hands; thy name
  Did thorns for frontlet stamp between Mine eyes.
I, Holy One, put on thy guilt and shame;
  I, God, Priest, Sacrifice.

A thief upon My right hand and My left;
  Six hours alone, athirst, in misery:
At length, in death, one smote My heart, and cleft

A hiding place for thee.

Nailed to the racking cross, than bed of down
    More dear, whereon to stretch Myself and sleep;
So did I win a kingdom—share My crown;
    A harvest—come and reap.

—CHRISTINA GEORGINA ROSSETTI

My God, my God, why hast Thou forsaken Me?

PSALM 22:1

And at the ninth hour Jesus cried with a loud voice, saying, Eloi, Eloi, lama sabachthani? which is, being interpreted, My God, my God, why hast Thou forsaken Me?

MARK 15:34

A Prayer to Prepare for Death

A surrender, which I know thou wilt accept, whether I live or die; for thy servant David made it, when he put himself into thy protection for his life; and thy blessed Son made it, when he delivered up his soul at his death; declare thou thy will upon me, O Lord, for life or death, in thy time; receive my surrender of myself, now: Into thy hands, O Lord, I commend my spirit. And being thus, O my God, prepared by thy correction, mellowed by thy chastisement, and conformed to thy will, by thy Spirit, having received thy pardon for my soul, and asking no reprieve for my Body, I am bold, O Lord, to bend my prayers to thee, for his assistance, the voice of whose bell hath called me to this devotion. Lay hold upon his soul, O God, till that soul have thoroughly considered his account, and how few minutes it have to remain in that body, let the power of thy Spirit recompense the shortness of time, and perfect his account, before he pass away: present his sins so to him, as that he may know what thou forgive, and not doubt of thy forgiveness; let him stop upon the infiniteness of those sins, but dwell upon the infiniteness of thy Mercy: let him discern his own demerits, but wrap himself up in the merits of thy Son, Christ Jesus: Breathe inward comforts to his heart, and afford him the power of giving such outward testimonies thereof, as all that are about him may derive comforts from thence, and have this edification, even in this dissolution, that though the body be going the way of all flesh, yet that soul is going the way of all Saints.

When thy Son cried out upon the Cross, My God, my God, Why hast thou forsaken me? he spoke not so much in his own Person, as in the person of the Church, and of his afflicted members, who in deep distresses might fear thy forsaking. This patient, O most blessed God, is one of them, in his behalf, and in his name, hear thy Son crying to thee, My God, my God, why hast thou forsaken me? and forsake him not; but with thy left hand lay his body in the grave (if that be thy determination upon him) and with thy right hand receive his soul into thy Kingdom, and unite him and us in one Communion of Saints. Amen.

—JOHN DONNE

Now there stood by the cross of Jesus His mother, and His mother's sister, Mary the wife of Cleophas, and Mary Magdalene. When Jesus therefore saw His mother, and the disciple standing by, whom He loved, He saith unto His mother, Woman, behold thy son! Then saith He to the disciple, Behold thy mother! And from that hour that disciple took her unto his own home. After this, Jesus knowing that all things were now accomplished, that the scripture might be fulfilled, saith, I thirst. Now there

was set a vessel full of vinegar: and they filled a spunge with vinegar, and put it upon hyssop, and put it to His mouth. When Jesus therefore had received the vinegar, He said, It is finished: and He bowed His head, and gave up the ghost.

JOHN 19:25—30

Good Friday

Am I a stone and not a sheep
    That I can stand, O Christ, beneath Thy Cross,
    To number drop by drop Thy Blood's slow loss,
And yet not weep?

Not so those women loved
    Who with exceeding grief lamented Thee;
    Not so fallen Peter weeping bitterly;
Not so the thief was moved;

Not so the Sun and Moon
    Which hid their faces in a starless sky,
A horror of great darkness at broad noon,—
    I, only I.

Yet give not o'er.
    But seek Thy sheep, true Shepherd of the flock;
Greater than Moses, turn and look once more
    And smite a rock.

—CHRISTINA GEORGINA ROSSETTI

GOSPEL

Mary at the Cross

Now there stood by the cross of Jesus his Mother.

O wondrous Mother! since the dawn of time
  Was ever love, was ever grief, like thine?
O highly favored in thy joy's deep flow,
  And favored even in this, thy bitterest woe!

Poor was that home in simple Nazareth
  Where, fairly growing, like some silent flower,
Last of a kingly race, unknown and lowly,
  O desert lily, passed thy childhood's hour.

The world knew not the tender, serious maiden,
  Who through deep loving years so silent grew,
Full of high thought and holy aspiration,
  Which the o'ershadowing God alone might view.

And then it came, that message from the highest,
  Such as to woman ne'er before descended,
The Almighty wings thy prayerful soul o'erspread,
  And with thy life the Life of worlds was blended.

What visions then of future glory filled thee,
  The chosen mother of the King unknown,
Mother fulfiller of all prophecy
  Which through dim ages wondering seers had
    shown!

Well did thy dark eye kindle, thy deep soul
  Rise into billows, and thy heart rejoice;

Then woke the poet's fire, the prophet's song,
    Tuned with strange burning words thy timid
      voice.

Then, in dark contrast, came the lowly manger,
    The outcast shed, the tramp of brutal feet;
Again behold earth's learned and her lowly,
    Sages and shepherds prostrate at thy feet.

Then to the temple bearing, hark again
    What strange conflicting tones of prophecy
Breathe o'er the child, foreshadowing words of joy,
    High triumph blent with bitter agony!

O, highly favored thou in many an hour
    Spent in lone musings with thy wondrous Son!
When thou didst gaze into that glorious eye,
    And hold that mighty hand within thine own.

Blest through those thirty years, when in thy dwelling
    He lived a God disguised with unknown power;
And thou his sole adorer, his best love,
    Trusting, revering, waited for his hour.

Blest in that hour when called by opening heaven
    With cloud and voice, and the baptizing flame,
Up from the Jordan walked the acknowledged
      stranger,
    And awestruck crowds grew silent as he came.

Blessed, when full of grace, with glory crowned,
    He from both hands almighty favors poured,

GOSPEL

And though He had not where to lay his head,
　　Brought to his feet alike the slave and lord.

Crowds followed; thousands shouted, "Lo, our
　　King!"
　　Fast beat thy heart. Now, now the hour draws
　　nigh:
Behold the crown, the throne, the nations bend!
　　Ah, no! fond mother, no! Behold him die!

Now by that cross thou tak'st thy final station,
　　And shar'st the last dark trial of thy Son;
Not with weak tears or woman's lamentation,
　　But with high silent anguish like his own.

Hail! highly favored, even in this deep passion;
　　Hail! in this bitter anguish thou art blest,—
Blest in the holy power with him to suffer
　　Those deep death-pangs that lead to higher rest.

All now is darkness; and in that deep stillness
　　The God-man wrestles with that mighty woe;
Hark to that cry, the rock of ages rending,—
　　"Tis finished!" Mother, all is glory now!

By sufferings mighty as his mighty soul,
　　Hath the Redeemer risen forever blest;
And through all ages must his heart-beloved
　　Through the same baptism enter the same rest.

—Harriet Beecher Stowe

CRUCIFIXION

Now there was set a vessel full of vinegar: and they filled a sponge with vinegar, and put it upon hyssop, and put it to His mouth. When Jesus therefore had received the vinegar, He said, It is finished: and He bowed His head, and gave up the ghost.

JOHN 19:29–30

His Saviour's Words, Going to the Cross

Have, have ye no regard, all ye
Who pass this way, to pity me,
Who am a man of misery!

A man both bruis'd, and broke, and one
Who suffers not here for mine own,
But for my friends' transgression!

Ah! Zion's Daughters, do not fear
The Cross, the Cords, the Nails, the Spear,
The Myrrh, the Gall, the Vineger:
For Christ, your loving Saviour, hath
Drunk up the wine of God's fierce wrath;
Only, there's left a little froth,

Less for to taste, than for to show,
What bitter cups had been your due,
Had He not drank them up for you.

—ROBERT HERRICK

*And as Peter was beneath in the palace, there
cometh one of the maids of the high priest: And
when she saw Peter warming himself, she looked
upon him, and said, And thou also wast with Jesus
of Nazareth. But he denied, saying, I know not,
neither understand I what thou sayest. And he went
out into the porch; and the cock crew. And a maid
saw him again, and began to say to them that stood
by, This is one of them. And he denied it again. And
a little after, they that stood by said again to Peter,
Surely thou art one of them: for thou art a
Galilaean, and thy speech agreeth thereto. But he
began to curse and to swear, saying, I know not this
man of whom ye speak. And the second time the
cock crew. And Peter called to mind the word that
Jesus said unto him, Before the cock crow twice,
thou shalt deny me thrice. And when he thought
thereon, he wept.*

MARK 14:66–72

In the Servants' Quarters

"Man, you too, aren't you, one of these rough
followers of the criminal?
All hanging hereabout to gather how he's going to
bear
Examination in the hall." She flung disdainful
glances on

The shabby figure standing at the fire with others there,
    Who warmed them by its flare.

"No, indeed, my skipping maiden: I know nothing of the trial here,
Or criminal, if so he be.—I chanced to come this way,
And the fire shone out into the dawn, and morning airs are cold now;
I, too, was drawn in part by charms I see before me play,
    That I see not every day."

"Ha, ha!" then laughed the constables who also stood to warm themselves,
The while another maiden scrutinized his features hard,
As the blaze threw into contrast every line and knot that wrinkled them,
Exclaiming, "Why, last night when he was brought in by the guard,
    You were with him in the yard!"

"Nay, nay, you teasing wench, I say! You know you speak mistakenly,
Cannot a tired pedestrian who has legged it long and far
Here on his way from northern parts, engrossed in humble marketings,
Come in and rest awhile, although judicial doings are
    Afoot by morning star?"

Gospel

"O come, come!" laughed the constables. "Why,
man, you speak the dialect
He uses in his answers; you can hear him up the stairs.
So own it. We sha'n't hurt ye. There he's speaking
now! His syllables
Are those you sound yourself when you are talking
unawares,

    As the pretty girl declares."

"And you shudder when his chain clinks!" she
rejoined. "O yes, I noticed it.
And you winced, too, when those cuffs they gave
him echoed to us here.
They'll soon be coming down, and you may then
have to defend yourself
Unless you hold your tongue, or go away and keep
you clear

    When he's led to judgment near!"

"No, I'll be damned in hell if I know anything
about the man!
No single thing about him more than everybody
knows.
Must not I even warm my hands but I am charged
with blasphemies?" . . .
—His face convulses as the morning cock that
moment crows,
And he droops, and turns, and goes.

                   —Thomas Hardy

And after this Joseph of Arimathaea, being a disciple of Jesus, but secretly for fear of the Jews, besought Pilate that he might take away the body of Jesus: and Pilate gave him leave. He came therefore, and took the body of Jesus. And there came also Nicodemus, which at the first came to Jesus by night, and brought a mixture of myrrh and aloes, about an hundred pound weight. Then took they the body of Jesus, and wound it in linen clothes with the spices, as the manner of the Jews is to bury. Now in the place where He was crucified there was a garden; and in the garden a new sepulchre, wherein was never man yet laid. There laid they Jesus therefore because of the Jews' preparation day; for the sepulchre was nigh at hand.

JOHN 19:38–42

Barnfloor and Winepress

Thou who on Sin's wages starvest,
Behold we have the Joy of Harvest:
For us was gathered the First-fruits,
For us was lifted from the roots,
Sheaved in cruel bands, bruised sore,
Scourged upon the threshing floor,
Where the upper millstone roofed His Head,
At morn we found the Heavenly Bread;
And on a thousand altars laid,

GOSPEL

Christ our Sacrifice is made.

Thou, whose dry plot for moisture gapes,
We shout with them that tread the grapes;
For us the Vine was fenced with thorn,
Five ways the precious branches torn.
Terrible fruit was on the tree
In the acre of Gethsemane:
For us by Calvary's distress
The wine was racked from the press;
Now, in our altar-vessels stored,
Lo, the sweet vintage of the Lord!

In Joseph's garden they threw by
The riven Vine, leafless, lifeless, dry:
On Easter morn the Tree was forth,
In forty days reached Heaven from earth,
Soon the whole world is overspread:
Ye weary, come into the shade.
The field where He hath planted us
Shall shake her fruit as Libanus,
When He has sheaved us in His sheaf,
When He had made us bear His leaf,
We scarcely call that banquet food,
But even our Saviour's and our blood,
We are so grafted on His wood.

—GERARD MANLEY HOPKINS

And he bought fine linen, and took Him down, and wrapped Him in the linen, and laid Him in a sepulchre which was hewn out of a rock, and rolled a stone unto the door of the sepulchre.

MARK 15:46

Upon Our Savior's Tomb Wherein Never Man Was Laid

How Life and Death in thee
    Agree!
Thou hadst a virgin Womb
    And Tomb.
A Joseph did betroth
    Them both.

—RICHARD CRASHAW

And when the sabbath was past, Mary Magdalene, and Mary the mother of James, and Salome, had bought sweet spices, that they might come and anoint Him.

MARK 16:1

Mary Magdalene and the Other Mary

Our Master lies asleep and is at rest:
    His heart has ceased to bleed, his eye to weep:
The sun ashamed has dropped down in the west;
    Our Master lies asleep.

Now we are they who weep, and trembling keep
    Vigil, with wrung heart in a sighing breast,
While slow time creeps, and slow the shadows creep.
Renew thy youth, as eagle from the nest;
    O Master, who hast sown, arise to reap;—
No cock-crow yet, no flush on eastern crest;
    Our Master lies asleep

                   —CHRISTINA GEORGINA ROSSETTI

THE RESURRECTION

He is not here, but is risen: remember how He spake unto you when He was yet in Galilee . . .

Luke 24:6

Easter

Most glorious Lord of life that on this day
 Didst make Thy triumph over death and sin,
And having harrowed hell didst bring away
 Captivity thence captive us to win;
 This joyous day, dear Lord, with joy begin
And grant that we, for whom Thou didest die
 Being with Thy dear blood clean washed from sin,
May live forever in felicity.
And that Thy love we weighing worthily,

May likewise love Thee for the same again;
And for Thy sake that all like dear didst buy,
    With love may one another entertain.
So let us love, dear love, like as we ought,
Love is the lesson which the Lord us taught.

—EDMUND SPENSER

*And the angel answered and said unto the women,
Fear not ye: for I know that ye seek Jesus, which
was crucified. He is not here: for He is risen, as He
said. Come, see the place where the Lord lay. And
go quickly, and tell His disciples that He is risen
from the dead; and, behold, He goeth before you
into Galilee; there shall ye see Him: lo, I have told
you.*

MATTHEW 28:5—7

Christ Is Arisen

Christ is arisen.
    Joy to thee, mortal!
Out of His prison,
    Forth from its portal!
Christ is not sleeping,
    Seek Him no longer;

Strong was His keeping,
    Jesus was stronger.

Christ is arisen.
    Seek Him not here;
Lonely His prison,
    Empty His bier;
Vain His entombing,
    Spices and lawn,
Vain the perfuming,
    Jesus is gone.

Christ is arisen.
    Joy to thee, mortal!
Empty His prison,
    Broken its portal!
Rising, He giveth
    His shroud to the sod;
Risen, He liveth,
    And liveth to God.

—J. W. VON GOETHE

Seven Stanzas at Easter

Make no mistake
if he rose at all
it was as his body;
if the cells' dissolution did not reverse, the

molecules reknit, the amino acids rekindle,
the church will fall.

It was not as the flowers,
each soft Spring recurrent;
it was not as his Spirit in the mouths and
    fuddled eyes of the eleven apostles;
it was as his flesh: ours.

The same hinged thumbs and toes,
the same valved heart
that—pierced—died, withered, decayed, and then
    regathered out of his Father's might
new strength to enclose.

Let us not mock God with metaphor,
analogy, sidestepping transcendence;
making of the event a parable, a sign painted in the
    faded credulity of earlier ages;
let us walk through the door.

The stone is rolled back, not papier mache,
not a stone in a story,
but the vast rock of materiality that in the slow
    grinding of time will eclipse each of us
the wide light of day.

And if we will have an angel at the tomb,
make it a real angel,
weighty with Max Planck's quanta, vivid with hair,
    opaque in the dawn light, robed in real linen

spun on a definite loom.

Let us not seek to make it less monstrous,
for our own convenience, our own sense of beauty,
lest, awakened in one unthinkable hour, we are
    embarrassed by the miracle,
and crushed by remonstrance.

—JOHN UPDIKE

*And, behold, two of them went that same day to a
village called Emmaus, which was from Jerusalem
about threescore furlongs. And they talked together of all these things which had happened. And it
came to pass, that, while they communed together
and reasoned, Jesus himself drew near, and went
with them. But their eyes were holden that they
should not know Him. And He said unto them,
What manner of communications are these that ye
have one to another, as ye walk, and are sad? And
the one of them, whose name was Cleopas, answering said unto Him, Art thou only a stranger in
Jerusalem, and hast not known the things which
are come to pass there in these days? And He said
unto them, What things? And they said unto Him,
Concerning Jesus of Nazareth, which was a
prophet mighty in deed and word before God and
all the people: And how the chief priests and our
rulers delivered Him to be condemned to death, and*

have crucified Him. But we trusted that it had been He which should have redeemed Israel: and beside all this, today is the third day since these things were done. Yea, and certain women also of our company made us astonished, which were early at the sepulchre; And when they found not His body, they came, saying, that they had also seen a vision of angels, which said that He was alive. And certain of them which were with us went to the sepulchre, and found it even so as the women had said: but Him they saw not. Then He said unto them, O fools, and slow of heart to believe all that the prophets have spoken: Ought not Christ to have suffered these things, and to enter into His glory? And beginning at Moses and all the prophets, He expounded unto them in all the scriptures the things concerning Himself. And they drew nigh unto the village, whither they went: and He made as though He would have gone further. But they constrained Him, saying, Abide with us: for it is toward evening, and the day is far spent. And He went in to tarry with them. And it came to pass, as He sat at meat with them, He took bread, and blessed it, and brake, and gave to them. And their eyes were opened, and they knew Him; and He vanished out of their sight. And they said one to another, Did not our heart burn within us, while He talked with us by the way, and while He opened to us the scriptures? And they rose up the same hour, and returned to Jerusalem, and found the eleven gathered together, and them that were with

them, Saying, The Lord is risen indeed, and hath
appeared to Simon. And they told what things were
done in the way, and how He was known of them
in breaking of bread.

LUKE 24:13—35

The Walk to Emmaus

It happened, on a solemn eventide,
Soon after he that was our surety died,
Two bosom friends, each pensively inclined,
The scene of all those sorrows left behind,
Sought their own village, busied, as they went,
In musings worthy of the great event:
They spake of him they loved, of him whose life,
Though blameless, had incurred perpetual strife,
Whose deeds had left, in spite of hostile arts,
A deep memorial graven on their hearts.
The recollection, like a vein of ore,
The farther traced, enriched them still the more;
They thought him, and they justly thought him, one
Sent to do more than He appeared t'have done;
To exalt a people, and to place them high
Above all else, and wondered he should die.
Ere yet they brought their journey to an end,
A Stranger joined them, courteous as a friend,
And asked them, with a kind engaging air,
What their affliction was, and begged a share.
Informed, he gathered up the broken thread,

GOSPEL

And, truth and wisdom gracing all he said,
Explained, illustrated, and searched so well
The tender theme, on which they chose to dwell,
That reaching home, "The night," they said, "is near,
We must not now be parted, sojourn here."
The new acquaintance soon became a guest,
And, made so welcome at their simple feast,
He blessed the bread, but vanished at the word,
And left them both exclaiming, "'Twas the Lord!
Did not our hearts feel all he deigned to say,
Did they not burn within us by the way?"

—WILLIAM COWPER

But Thomas, one of the twelve, called Didymus, was not with them when Jesus came. The other disciples therefore said unto him, We have seen the Lord. But he said unto them, Except I shall see in His hands the print of the nails, and put my finger into the print of the nails, and thrust my hand into His side, I will not believe.

JOHN 20:24—25

THE RESURRECTION

St. Thomas

Ah! Thomas, wherefore wouldst thou doubt,
  And put the Lord in pain,
And mad'st his wounds to spout
  Anew from every vein?

Lo! those of God are blessed most,
  Which, simple and serene,
Believe the Holy Ghost,
  That operates unseen.

This is that great and prior proof
  Of God and of his Son,
Beneath whose sacred roof
  To-day the duty's done.

Though seventeen hundred years remote,
  We can perform our part,
And to the Lord devote
  The tribute of our heart.

O Lord, the slaves of sin release,
  Their ways in Christ amend,
Our faith and hope increase,
  Our charities extend.

Make thou our altered lives of use
  To all the skirts around.
And purge from each abuse
  Thy church, so much renowned.

Enlarge from Mammon's spells her priests,
    And from all carnal cares,
And bid to ghostly feasts,
    To pure cherubic airs.

Thy people in that choir employ
    Whose business is above,
In gratitude and joy,
    In wonder, praise, and love.

—Christopher Smart

And after eight days again His disciples were within, and Thomas with them: then came Jesus, the doors being shut, and stood in the midst, and said, Peace be unto you. Then saith He to Thomas, Reach hither thy finger, and behold My hands; and reach hither thy hand, and thrust it into My side: and be not faithless, but believing. And Thomas answered and said unto Him, My Lord and my God. Jesus saith unto him, Thomas, because thou hast seen Me, thou hast believed: blessed are they that have not seen, and yet have believed.

John 20:26–29

Split the Lark—and You'll Find the Music

Split the Lark—and you'll find the Music—
Bulb after Bulb, in Silver rolled—
Scantily dealt to the Summer Morning
Saved for your Ear when Lutes be old.

Loose the Flood—you shall find it patent—
Gush after Gush, reserved for you—
Scarlet Experiment! Sceptic Thomas!
Now, do you doubt that your Bird was true?

—EMILY DICKINSON

And it came to pass, while He blessed them, He was parted from them, and carried up into heaven. And they worshipped Him, and returned to Jerusalem with great joy: And were continually in the temple, praising and blessing God. Amen.

LUKE 24:51—53

Ascension

Salute the last and everlasting day.
Joy at the uprising of this Sun, and Son,
Ye whose just tears, or tribulation

Have purely washed, or burnt your drossie clay;
Behold the Highest, parting hence away,
Lightens the dark clouds, which he treads upon,
Nor doth he by ascending, show alone,
But first he, and he first enters the way.
O strong Ram, which hast batter'd heaven for me,
Mild lamb, which with thy blood, hast mark'd the
    path;
Bright Torch, which shin'st, that I the way may see,
Oh, with thy own blood quench thy own just wrath,
And if thy holy Spirit, my Muse did raise,
Deign at my hands this crown of prayer and praise.

—JOHN DONNE

*R*emember!—It is Christianity "To Do Good," always—even to those who do evil to us. It is Christianity to love our neighbours as ourself, and to do to all men as we would have them do to us. It is Christianity to be gentle, merciful, and forgiving, and to keep those qualities quiet in our own hearts, and never make a boast of them, or of our prayers or of our love of God but always to show that we love Him by humbly trying to do right in everything. If we do this, and remember the life and lessons of Our Lord Jesus Christ, and try to act up to them, we may confidently hope that God will forgive us our sins and mistakes, and enable us to live and die in peace.

—CHARLES DICKENS

Biographical Notes

Matthew Arnold (1822–1888) was the preeminient literary critic of Victorian England, with a pervasive influence that reflected his strong spiritual and ethical convictions. Arnold was also a celebrated poet ("Dover Beach" is best remembered today), winning prizes for verse at a very young age. After college, however, to support his family, he took a job as inspector of schools—and held the post for thirty-five years, exerting a positive influence on British education as he had on British letters.

W. H. Auden (1907–1973) is considered one of the most significant poets of the twentieth century. As an Oxford student, he joined a group of young leftist writers, among them Stephen Spender and Christopher Isherwood. Wanting to oppose the Fascists during the Spanish Civil War, Auden volunteered as an ambulance driver. The poet emigrated to the United States in 1939, becoming a citizen in 1946. The postwar period also marks Auden's return to the Anglican Church of his youth and a Pulitzer Prize for poetry which embodies his renewed religious affirmation.

Charlotte Brontë (1816–1855) assisted in the education of her two younger sisters, Anne and Emily (though all three attended a school for clergymen's daughters). Asked at age seven by her father to name "the best book in the world," Charlotte answered, "The Bible." The Brontë girls read voraciously and had soaring imaginations, which led to an amazing literary output of novels and poems. Charlotte is beloved for her novel, *Jane Eyre*, Emily for *Wuthering Heights*, and Anne for tender hymns and poems.

Rupert Brooke (1887–1915) came to represent an entire generation of idealistic English youth that was lost, either in death or total disillusionment, in the First World War. Educated at Rugby and Cambridge, Brooke was as noted for his physical beauty as his intellectual gifts—"a golden young Apollo," was one appraisal. The young poet traveled extensively in Europe, North America, and the South Seas, before seeing war duty in Belgium and the Mediterranean. He died of fever on the Greek island of Skyros.

Elizabeth Barrett Browning (1806–1861) was not only a devotee of literature, but a scholar of Latin, Greek, Hebrew, French, German, and Italian. For years delicate health confined her to bed in a darkened room, where she wrote poetry to amuse herself. After these were published, through an exchange of ecstatic letters she fell in love with poet Robert Browning. They married in secret, against the wishes of her autocratic father, and fled to Italy. Their love affair is chronicled in her *Sonnets From the Portuguese*. Her poetry reflects the glory of spirituality and righteousness.

William Cullen Bryant (1794–1878), born in a farming village in Massachusetts, was schooled in Latin by his minister uncle and in Greek by another clergyman. Two months after learning the Greek alphabet, young Bryant read the New Testament. Although he studied law, he found success as an editor and journalist. His poems are remarkable for artistic and moral purity.

Lewis Carroll (1832–1898) was the pen name of Charles Lutwidge Dodgson, author of *Alice in Wonderland* and *Through the Looking Glass*, loved by generations of children—and adults. Dodgson, who always shied away from his pseudonymous fame, also had an unremarkable career as a lecturer in mathematics at Oxford. The son of a clergyman, Dodgson became an Anglican deacon at the age of twenty-nine. His father's old parsonage in Cheshire was later rebuilt with an added memorial window that showed "Carroll" and Alice kneeling with the shepherds in the stable at Bethlehem.

G. K. Chesterton (1874–1936) won a London schoolboy's "Milton" prize for splendid verse. The grownup Chesterton, however, earned his keep as a freelance journalist, reviewing books and working in a publisher's office, while churning out, fiction, poetry, and criticism. An interesting literary outgrowth of Chesterton's middle-aged conversion to Catholicism was the fictional Father Brown, who, in a celebrated series of crime novels, combines his sleuthing with sermonizing.

Samuel Taylor Coleridge (1772–1834) was raised at his father's vicarage in Devonshire, England. At three he could read the Bible, and then the Arabian Nights before he was five. An early plan to become a Unitarian minister was abandoned when he fell under the spell of opium (poems such as "Kubla Khan" mirror his drugged imagination). Coleridge recovered his Christian faith later in life and was esteemed as a great religious thinker. He died in communion with the Church of England.

William Cowper (1731–1800) was born in his father's rectory in Hertshire, England. When his mother died, Cowper was only six, so his father, who also served as chaplain to King George II, sent the boy off to boarding school. Beset by disabling attacks of melancholy all his life, Cowper managed, with the help of devoted family and friends, to produce a prolific amount of fine poetry and even finer correspondence. He has been described as "a good and pious man" and "a broken genius."

Richard Crashaw (1613–1649) was influenced by George Herbert to express his genius in religious verse. But the young man had inherited a passion both for theology and poetry from his clergyman father. During civil strife in England, Crashaw fled to France, where eventually, though raised a fierce "antipapist," he embraced Catholicism. His religious and secular poems were collected by a friend and published anonymously during his exile. The poet died in Italy at the age of thirty-six in the service of a cardinal.

E. E. Cummings (1894–1962) delighted in being the bad boy of American poetry. He was born in Cambridge, Massachusetts, where his father was a Harvard professor and an ordained minister. After his own Harvard studies, young Edward Estlin rushed off to Europe—World War I was breaking out—to serve in the ambulance corps. His first volume of poems, appearing when he was thirty, gained notoriety for its unusual rhythms and lack of uppercase letters. And yet, despite this linguistic and typographical playfulness, Cummings' poetry betrays his Unitarian and Transcendental heritage—and ultimately celebrates a vision of a redeemed world.

Charles Dickens (1812–1870) passed part of his childhood at his father's side in debtors' prison, and from age ten till twelve he was forced to work in a blacking factory. These distressing experiences were used later to powerful effect, particularly in his novels *Little Dorritt* and *David Copperfield*. His poignant fable of repentance, *A Christmas Carol*, has become synonymous with the season of the Nativity. Less well known is a little volume he penned for his children, *The Life of Our Lord*. Though not averse to skewering hypocrisy in the church (or elsewhere), Dickens felt an affinity for Anglican Christianity. In his will, he commended his soul to God and the mercy of Jesus Christ.

Emily Dickinson (1830–1886) died in the house where she was born in Amherst, Massachusetts, a profoundly Christian New England town. After brief schooling, she settled into seclusion, probably because of an unhappy love affair, which she ended because she could not "wreck another woman's life." Almost completely withdrawn from life, Emily would not allow family and friends to publish her poetry during her lifetime. After Emily's death, her sister found more than a thousand poems hidden in boxes and drawers, some in hand-stitched booklets, others penned on the backs of old envelopes and shopping lists. These ingenious works reflect a mystical love of God. Her life was celebrated in the 1976 play, *The Belle of Amherst.*

John Donne (1572–1631) was born into a family of staunch Catholics, with two Jesuit uncles. But when he came of age, he rejected Catholicism to embrace the Anglican Church. In straitened circumstances, with a sickly wife and seven children, he was pressured by King James to take religious orders. His first sermon before the king reportedly carried his audience "to heaven, in holy raptures." His poems reflect the struggle between spirit and flesh, individual faith and general disillusionment.

T. S. Eliot (1888–1965), born in St. Louis, Missouri, to a distinguished Boston family that founded Washington University, stayed on in England after his Oxford years. His ingenious poetry, especially after publication of "The Waste Land," created a literary sensation on both sides of Atlantic; and ultimately won him the Nobel Prize. After 1927, when Eliot became a British subject and joined the Anglican church, his poems and plays reflected his search for spiritual meaning, with frequent allusions to religious literature. As Ezra Pound once chided, Eliot began to prefer "Moses to the Muses."

Robert Frost (1874–1963) was born in San Francisco, though his ancestry was strictly New

England. After his father's death when Frost was only ten, his mother returned east to settle in Lawrence, Massachusetts. A poet herself with deep religious convictions, she nurtured her son's poetic gifts and fostered the rich vein of mysticism and symbolism that permeates his "talky" blank verse. Before Frost's "overnight success" arrived in his forties, he'd tried his hand at teaching school, making shoes, editing a weekly paper, and farming. Winner of four Pulitzer Prizes, Frost has been described as the purest classical poet of America.

Johann Wolfgang von Goethe (1749–1832) had a passion for poetry as early as age eight. At nine he built an altar and developed his own mystical religion, in hopes of approaching God directly. At thirteen he studied Hebrew and read much of the Bible, while his secular studies encompassed literature, science, law, medicine—indeed, the whole of human learning. At the University of Leipzig young Goethe wrote verses in German, French, English, and Italian. He went on to achieve such international eminence with his voluminous works that Thomas Carlyle proclaimed him "the teacher and exemplar of his age."

Robert Graves (1895–1985), a poet-scholar who produced 150 books and 800 essays and poems over seven decades, was best known at the end of his long life for the BBC's TV adaptation of his historical novel, *I, Claudius*. He was born in London,

the son of an Irish educator. After nearly dying in
the trenches during World War I, Graves graduated
from Oxford, married and took a teaching post at
the University of Cairo. Most of the rest of his life
was spent abroad, especially on the Spanish island
of Majorca where he died at the age of ninety.
Despite his prodigious output of fiction, biographies, scholarly essays, and translations, poetry
remained Graves' abiding passion.

Thomas Hardy (1840–1928), overcoming early
rejection, went on to achieve both literary and popular acclaim for his compelling novels, among them
Tess of the D'Urbervilles and *Far From the
Madding Crowd* (both made into movies). But the
hostile reception accorded *Jude the Obscure* sent
him back to epic and lyric poetry, which he had
long preferred. Interestingly, Hardy's family had
prepared him for a quite different career. At sixteen
he was apprenticed to an ecclesiastical architect, for
whom he sketched and measured many old churches
in his hometown of Dorset, England.

Nathaniel Hawthorne (1804–1864), born in Salem,
Massachusetts embodied the spirit of the New
England school of letters. His father, a sea captain
like his father before him, died when Hawthorne
was just a child, and his strict Puritan mother raised
her family under meager and gloomy circumstances. Hawthorne brooded as an artist, laboring
over his style in short stories and poetry. Despite

being championed by such eminent friends as Ralph Waldo Emerson and Edgar Allan Poe, Hawthorne was convinced he would continue in literary obscurity. Then, at the age of forty-six, *The Scarlet Letter*, which embodies his deep ethical concerns, became an unlikely popular success. Hawthorne solidified his reputation with *The House of Seven Gables*.

George Herbert (1593–1633) was profoundly influenced by his mother, a friend of John Donne. Herbert taught briefly at Cambridge, where he had been educated. When an attempt to succeed at court failed, however, he determined "to lose himself in an humble way" and take priestly orders. He loved the Church of England and held services twice a day at his parish in Salisbury. Like his mentor, Donne, Herbert found spiritual inspiration in everyday objects. He is noted for his pious and playful poetry.

Robert Herrick (1591–1674) was the son of a London goldsmith. He took a small vicarage near Devonshire and celebrated the rural customs in his village. Though his sermons were termed "florid and witty," Herrick, who never married, is far better known for his pastoral love poems.

Gerard Manley Hopkins (1844–1889) was born into a High Anglican family, but converted to Roman Catholicism at age twenty-two. Two years later he became a Jesuit and burned many of his spiritual-sensual poems, believing the religious life incompatible with creating poetry. Fortunately, much of his innovative work survived, allowing us to experience the depth and passion of his religious convictions.

A. E. Housman (1859-1936) was born in Worcestershire, England, near the Shropshire country depicted so vividly in his poems. A cloistered classical scholar at Cambridge, Housman surprised many academic colleagues with publication of "A Shropshire Lad." Though clearly composed in the pastoral tradition, with echoes of Scottish border ballads and Shakespearan songs, these memorable verses also betray a strong biblical influence, often utilizing language from the Old and New Testaments.

Ben Jonson (1572–1637), though raised by a bricklayer stepfather, went on to receive honorary degrees from both Oxford and Cambridge. He possessed a great lyric gift ("Drink to Me Only With Thine Eyes" is one of his verses), but his real love was the theater, where he both wrote and performed (along with Shakespeare). In 1598 Jonson was arrested for killing a fellow actor in a duel, and while in prison converted to Roman Catholicism. His flirtation with Rome ended in 1610, and he returned to the Church of England. He died penniless but was buried with honors in Westminster Abbey.

Joyce Kilmer (1886–1918) was an accomplished journalist who worked for *The New York Times*, though he (not she) is chiefly remembered for his tender verse. A staunch Catholic, Kilmer found the beauty of poetry "not far from prayer and adoration." He was killed in France during World War I, attacking a German machine-gun nest.

Rudyard Kipling (1865–1936) was born in Bombay and educated in English boarding schools. He returned to India at seventeen to take up journalism. Early verse made him popular, but his witty and worldly short stories, collected in *Plain Tales From the Hills*, created a literary sensation in 1890s London. "Kipling is too clever to live," was Robert Louis Stevenson's admiring verdict. Though often criticized for celebrating British imperialism, Kipling has never been neglected. His classics—like the *Jungle Books* and *Captains Courageous*—delight generation after generation. He was awarded the 1907 Nobel Prize.

Charles Lamb (1775–1834) labored for thirty-three years as an accountant in the East India House, but what he called his "true works" were poems, essays and criticisms. In 1796 his sister Mary, in a manic state, stabbed their mother to death. Rather than have Mary incarcerated in an asylum, Charles took charge of her in what became a lifelong commitment. Together they wrote *Tales Founded on the Plays of Shakespeare* and *Poetry for Children*.

BIOGRAPHICAL NOTES

D. H. Lawrence (1885–1930) was born to a working-class family in Nottinghamshire, England, the fourth child of a coal miner. His youthful struggles to escape the mines through education are depicted in his autobiographical novel, *Sons and Lovers*. Despite ill health (he died of tuberculosis at forty-four) and endless wanderings with his wife, Frieda, Lawrence produced several novels, including the scandalous *Lady Chatterley's Lover*, as well as volumes on psychological and religious speculation. A complex and tortured man, Lawrence used his poetry to examine sensual and spiritual perplexities.

Henry Wadsworth Longfellow (1807–1882) was born in Portland, Maine, to a generations-old New England family. As a boy he wrote prose and verse for newspapers and magazines, but, when his father frowned on his literary aspirations, he pursued an academic career in modern languages. Paramount among his many translations from European poets is his rendering of Dante's *Divine Comedy*. Ultimately, in spite of his father's skepticism, Longfellow attained renown for his own literary works, especially such narrative poems as "Hiawatha," "The Courtship of Miles Standish," and "Paul Revere's Ride." He was the first American poet to receive a memorial in London's Westminster Abbey.

James Russell Lowell (1819–1891) succeeded Longfellow as professor of modern languages at

Harvard. Born in Cambridge, Massachusetts, the son of a Unitarian minister, Lowell began his studies with a law degree in mind, but turned to versifying in the tradition of John Keats. A considerable figure in his time, the professor-poet was also a skilled essayist, founding editor of the *Atlantic Monthly*, and, in his later years, a diplomat.

Robert Lowell (1917–1977), the great-grandson of James Russell Lowell, was Boston-born and Harvard-educated. Though raised in the Puritan tradition, Lowell in his early twenties embraced Roman Catholicism. His verse was frequently crafted to comment on national affairs, as were his public stances. He was a conscientious objector in World War II and a prominent protester during the Vietnam War. Lowell won two Pulitzer Prizes for his poetry and was regarded by many as the greatest American poet of his generation.

Andrew Marvell (1621–1678) was born in his father's rectory (and grammar school) in Yorkshire, England, educated there and at Trinity College. Known in his time more as a political satirist and pamphleteer, Marvell wrote "metaphysical" and "garden" poems that were circulated mostly in manuscript. When Milton was appointed Latin secretary under Oliver Cromwell, the great poet made Marvell his assistant. Marvell subsequently wrote an ode hailing Cromwell as Caesar, then adroitly changed his politics during the Restoration.

Marvell's poetic standing was improved more than a century after his death, thanks to the praise of William Wordsworth and Charles Lamb.

Thomas Merton (1915–1968) was born in France of artistic parents; his New Zealander father painted landscapes, his American mother studied interior design. Young Merton was schooled in France, England, and eventually at Columbia University in New York, under Mark Van Doren and Joseph Wood Krutch. In his early twenties he converted to Catholicism and three years later became a Trappist monk. An early autobiography, *The Seven Storey Mountain*, established Merton as a major Catholic writer. His subjects thereafter ranged from the contemplative life and Eastern religions to social issues, such as economic injustice and nuclear war. More than sixty volumes of Merton's writings are currently in print in English.

Edna St. Vincent Millay (1892–1950) burst on to the American literary scene at the age of twenty, a Greenwich Village bohemian who infused conventional poetic forms with a contemporary spirit. Though a Vassar graduate, she was not the daughter of privilege. Millay's father abandoned the family when she was only seven. Her mother, a nurse, supported her three daughters and encouraged them to develop their creative talents. Millay went on to write fiction, several plays, and even an opera libretto, but it was her poetry, especially her masterful sonnets, that earned enduring acclaim. The Austerlitz, New York, farmhouse where she and her husband lived is a National Historic Landmark.

John Milton (1608–1674) entered Cambridge with the idea of becoming a clergyman but abandoned it because, he wrote, "tyranny had invaded" the Church of England. He afterward devoted himself to scholarship and literature. Though profoundly religious and a genuine Christian who valued (and studied) the Bible over all other books, Milton no longer attended church. His masterwork, *Paradise Lost*, published when he was nearly sixty, describes Satan and his fallen angels warring with God and His angelic host.

Blaise Pascal (1623–1662) was an original genius in science and mathematics. Restricted by his father to the study of ancient languages, the boy worked out the principles of geometry on his own—and soon drew the attention of the great mathematician, René Descartes. One of Pascal's scientific discoveries became the basis for modern hydraulics. Later in life, while visiting his sister in a convent, Pascal began to seek God and found Him in a dramatic mystical experience (an account of which he kept in an amulet sewn into his clothing). Pascal, who subsequently took monastic orders, declared that perfect knowledge comes only through Christian revelation.

Boris Pasternak (1890–1960) was awarded the 1958 Nobel Prize after the publication, and world-wide success, of *Doctor Zhivago*, a novel in the epic Russian tradition. The manuscript, which had been smuggled out of the Soviet Union, was viewed by the Communist Party as "counter-revolutionary," and the author was coerced into refusing the great prize. Pasternak's profound fiction and lyrical poetry had been suppressed for many years prior; he earned his literary living translating Goethe and Shakespeare into Russian. Pasternak continued to be isolated and vilified by the Soviet government until his death in 1960. His masterpiece was finally published in Russia in 1988.

Alexander Pope (1688–1744) was the son of devotedly Catholic parents. He was his own tutor—not only in English but in French, Italian, Latin, and Greek. He spent a dozen years on his famous translations of Homer's *Iliad* and *Odyssey*. At twenty-four he published a sacred poem, "Messiah." By twenty-five he was a fashionable poet and recognized wit, earning a prosperous living with his pen. His *Essay on Man* was a defense of religion on natural grounds. According to the priest who gave him the last rites, "Pope's mind was resigned and wrapt up in the love of God and man."

Francis Quarles (1592–1644) was born in Essex, England, and educated at Cambridge. He graduated thereafter from one lucrative post to another:

cupbearer to the Princess Elizabeth; secretary of the Primate of Ireland; official city chronologer (in which he succeeded Ben Jonson). The father of eighteen children, Quarles was equally prolific with his pen. He gained particular fame for *Emblems*, perhaps the most popular book of verse published in the seventeenth century. Concerned with the soul's struggle for salvation, each "emblem" consisted of an engraving, a biblical paraphrase, quotations from Church Fathers, and a four-line epigram.

Rainer Maria Rilke (1875–1926), a visionary Austrian poet, is esteemed more now than in his lifetime—and, according to W. H. Auden, more in English translation than in the original German. Born in Prague, educated there and in Munich, Rilke was a literary nomad, wandering across Europe. In France, he served a stint as secretary to the great sculptor Rodin. In Italy, inspired by pictures of the Annunciation and the Flight into Egypt, he wrote a cycle of poems on the "Life of the Virgin Mary." Rilke's chief works, "Duino Elegies" and "Sonnets to Orpheus," show flashes of exquisite lyricism.

Christina Georgina Rossetti (1830–1894) was so devoted to her High Anglican faith that she turned down a suitor who was "either not a Christian at all, or else he was a Christian of undefined or heterodox views." Committed to the heavenly Bridegroom, her solitary life produced a wealth of deeply spiritual creative works, marked by magical imagery, an angelic voice and a love for nature.

Dante Gabriel Rossetti (1828–1882) was born into an impoverished but highly cultured household. His father, an eccentric professor of Italian, had highly original views on the poet Dante. The sensitive boy became a painter as well as a poet. His poetess sister Christina was the model for Rossetti's graceful painting of the Virgin Mary.

Edmond Rostand (1868–1918), the son of a journalist in Marseille, studied law before succumbing to the temptations of poetry and drama. He was able to combine both literary forms in his heroic comedy, *Cyrano de Bergerac*—a play in verse and a classic of the modern theater. Before that great success, which eventually got Rostand elected to the French Academy, he had written a little drama tailored for the famous actress Sarah Bernhardt, *La Samaritaine*, about the woman of Samaria who encounters Jesus at the well.

Carl Sandburg (1878–1967) has been called the "Laureate of Industrial America" for poetry like "The People, Yes," "Chicago Poems," and "Smoke and Steel." Born and raised in Illinois, the son of a Swedish blacksmith, Sandburg traveled the boxcars of the Midwest as a harvest hand. He also worked as a dishwasher, salesman, advertising manager, and journalist. Like Robert Frost, who similarly celebrated the mystical in the commonplace, Sandburg wasn't known as a poet till about his fortieth year. But he lived almost fifty more, becoming a Pulitzer Prize-winning poet, biographer of Abraham Lincoln, and beloved troubadour of American folk songs.

Dorothy Sayers (1893–1957), only child of an Anglican clergyman and schoolmaster, was one of the first women to attain an Oxford degree. She made her name with detective novels, a dozen starring the erudite Lord Peter Wimsey. So popular and profitable were they, Sayers was able to devote the last two decades of her life to what she deemed the "literature of expression"—giving eloquent voice to her religious convictions. "The Man Born to Be King," first broadcast over the BBC and later published in England and America, dramatized the life of Christ in twelve episodes.

Albert Schweitzer (1875–1965) lived astonishing parallel lives—philosopher, theologian, physician, musician, clergyman, missionary, and writer—achieving eminence in all. Born in Alsace, educated in France and Germany, Schweitzer decided to devote his twenties to science, music, and the ministry, the remainder of his life to the service of humanity. Keeping to his timetable and his "reverence for life" philosophy, Schweitzer walked away from his career as an internationally acclaimed organist and Bach interpreter to begin medical studies. Seven years later he became a missionary doctor in French Equatorial Africa (now Gabon) and remained there a half-century till his death. Given the 1952 Nobel Peace Prize for his humanitarian work, Schweitzer used the money to expand his hospital and establish a leper colony.

William Shakespeare (1564–1616) was the English playwright and poet with an unsurpassed power of language. His masterful works hold up a mirror to mankind. Yet much of what we know of his life is recorded in the Stratford parish register—his birth, his marriage at eighteen, the births of his children, his death. As he looked forward to the next life, he wrote in his will: "I commend my soul into the hands of God my Creator, hoping and assuredly believing, through the only merits of Jesus Christ my Saviour, to be made partaker of life everlasting."

(Dame) Edith Sitwell (1887–1964) was born in Yorkshire, England, the daughter of a baronet. Her brothers, Osbert and Sacheverell, were also gifted writers, and all three were eccentrics in their writing and personas. An imposing six feet tall, the poetess dressed distinctively in medieval fashions. Ten years before her death, she became a Roman Catholic.

Christopher Smart (1722–1771) showed precocious gifts as a poet, earning the patronage of a wealthy family. Upon entry into Cambridge, however, the young man fell prey to drink and indebtedness—the twin plagues of his life. Becoming a fellow of his college in spite of his dissipations, Smart repeated his wasteful ways when he moved to London at age thirty. An attempt to "pray without ceasing," an extreme interpretation of Paul's advice to the Thessalonians, landed Smart in an asylum for two years. There, denied pen and paper, he scratched his most famous poem, "The Song of David," into the woodwork of his room. This ecstatic song, however, was omitted from collections of Smart's verse till rediscovery a century later by Robert Browning.

Stephen Spender (1909–1995), poet, critic and essayist, was one of the "Oxford poets" of the 1930s, with W. H. Auden and C. Day Lewis. In succeeding decades Spender became better known as the founder of the intellectual journals, *Horizon* and *Encounter*. In 1993, ten years after receiving his knighthood, the aging English Poet Laureate became embroiled in a literary controversy. He claimed that *While England Sleeps*, a novel by David Leavitt, plagiarized Spender's own 1951 autobiography, *World Within World*. Leavitt's novel was withdrawn and reissued with all offending material deleted.

Edmund Spenser (1552–1599), the son of a London clothmaker, wrote and translated verse as a boy. He possessed the supreme poetic gifts of melody, rhythm, and image, and is credited with crystallizing the forms and patterns of English verse. His masterwork, *The Faerie Queen*, is an elaborate allegory of twelve books (only six were completed), each narrating the exploits of a knight who symbolized one of the "morall vertues." Spenser was a sincere and militant Christian.

Robert Louis Stevenson (1850–1894), to please his father, first studied engineering, then the law, but abandoned both for his real love—literature. This "shocking" decision, and the questioning of strict Scots Presbyterian theology, led his father to brand the lad a "horrible atheist." Yet spiritual concerns infuse all Stevenson's writings—polished essays and travel pieces, tender children's poetry, beloved adventures like *Dr. Jekyll and Mr. Hyde* and *Treasure Island*. Especially eloquent are the household prayers written for his family's use in Samoa.

Harriet Beecher Stowe (1811–1896) was, said Abraham Lincoln, "the little lady who caused this great war." Stowe's passionate belief in the abolition of slavery was expressed in *Uncle Tom's Cabin*, reflecting her deeply religious views. Her father, a strict Calvinist, headed a theological seminary in Cincinnati, Ohio, where Harriet attended school and married a professor. Five of her six brothers became ministers.

Jonathan Swift (1667–1745) could read any chapter in the Bible by the age of five. Born in Dublin to an

English family, Swift was educated at Trinity College. In England at the age of twenty-seven, he became a clergyman. But prospects for clerical advancement were crippled by a satirical essay, "Tale of the Tub," which took deadly aim at insincerity in literature and religion. Undaunted, Swift continued to dip his pen in his vitriol. Even his children's classic, *Gulliver's Travels*, with its Lilliputians and Yahoos, is a thinly veiled satire on human shams and shortcomings.

Alfred, Lord Tennyson (1809–1892) was the fourth of twelve children. Their father, an English clergyman, was also a skillful poet who supervised his children's schooling. Tennyson wrote verse at a precociously early age, but passed much of his young manhood in poverty and melancholy. Only at the age of forty-one, when he was appointed Poet Laureate by Queen Victoria, did his reputation and the sales of his works soar. A devout and sensitive man, Tennyson said of his wife, "The peace of God came into my life before the altar when I wedded her."

Dylan Thomas (1914–1953), born in Swansea, Wales, launched his writing career as a reporter. But after winning a newspaper poetry contest, he devoted his life to producing poems, short stories, and plays. For the potent imagery that typifies his verses, he drew mainly from the Bible and Welsh folklore. Thomas was a brilliant reader of his own and others' poetry, but his personal life was turbulent, with recurrent bouts of alcoholism and depression. His self-diagnosis was more poetic: "I hold a beast, an angel and a madman in me."

Leo Tolstoy (1828–1910), at time of his death, was the pre-eminent man of letters in all the world. Yet, at the peak of his powers three decades before, he had renounced literature. The creator of *War and Peace* and *Anna Karenina* had spent the balance of his life in a search for moral and religious justification, not only studying the Gospels intensely but teaching them to the village children on his country estate.

Ivan Turgenev (1818–1883), born into a wealthy, landed family, was educated in Moscow, St. Petersburg, and Berlin, but took a civil service post until his deftly told tales of Russian peasant life created a literary stir. Later collected as *Sportsman's Sketches* and widely praised, these realistic stories were a clear indictment of serfdom. Czar Nicholas I reacted by having their author arrested and exiled to his estate for a year. But Turgenev continued to produce—short stories, poems, dramas, criticism, and his novelistic masterpiece, *Fathers and Sons*. His influence on Russian literature was immense. "[Turgenev's] conscience," wrote Ernest Renan, French author of a popular *Life of Jesus*, "was the conscience of a people."

Sigrid Undset (1882–1949) won international acclaim (and best-sellerdom) for *Kristin*

Lavransdotter, a saga of Scandinavian life in the Middle Ages. When the Nobel Prize followed, Undset donated the money to charity. But success had come exceedingly hard. At sixteen, after her archaeologist father died, Undset abandoned university dreams for secretarial work to help support her mother and two sisters. She wrote fiction at night, on weekends, and holidays, reading widely in Nordic and foreign literature, particularly studying the Brontës and Jane Austen. A midlife spiritual crisis turned Undset from agnosticism to Catholicism, something of a scandal in Lutheran-dominated Norway. An early opponent of the Nazis, she was forced to flee her homeland in April, 1940, when the Germans invaded. She spent the rest of the war in the United States, pleading the cause of her occupied country.

John Updike (1932–), known for his novels, short stories, and essays, is also a serious and talented poet. A recurring theme in all his writings is the dilemma of contemporary man, caught between the disparate demands of faith and reason. Updike is often identified with his cycle of novels chronicling the life of Rabbit Angstrom against the backdrop of a rapidly changing America. Two of these have won Pulitzers: *Rabbit Is Rich* in 1982, *Rabbit at Rest* in 1991. After graduating summa cum laude from Harvard, and studying briefly abroad, Updike achieved early success with his short stories in *The New Yorker*.

Henry Vaughan (1621–1695), British poet and mystic, was born into an ancient Welsh family. Sent to London to study law, the young man instead became a physician. He published his first secular poetry at the age of twenty-four, but later turned his attention to sacred subjects. In the preface to a book of spiritual poems, Vaughan thanked "the blessed man, Mr. George Herbert, whose holy life and verse gained many pious converts, of whom I am the least." His mystical view of nature affected William Wordsworth, who owned a copy of Vaughan's poems.

John Greenleaf Whittier (1807–1892) was so closely connected to his faith that he was called the "Quaker Poet." Because of his staunch religious beliefs, he was a bitter enemy of slavery and used his creative energy to fuel abolition. Along with anti-slavery and pastoral New England poetry, Whittier wrote many hymns that are sung to this day.

Thornton Wilder (1897–1975) was essentially a moralist in his plays, something traceable in part to his morally upright father and Presbyterian minister grandfather. His inspirational novel, *The Bridge of San Luis Rey*, earned him a Pulitzer at the age of thirty-one. *Our Town*, which opened in 1938, remains America's most produced play, a touching and tender look at small-town life in a fictional New Hampshire town. "I am not interested in the ephemeral," Wilder once said, but "in those things that repeat and repeat and repeat in the lives of the millions."

William Wordsworth (1770–1850) found his three years at Cambridge of little intellectual profit. While his family hoped he would become a minister, the thought of "vegetating on a paltry curacy" had little appeal for the young man. Yet much of his delicate and intimate poetry is absorbed with divinity—and a "communion with nature," which he discovered as a child. Bereft after the death of his brother John, Wordsworth returned to the Anglican Church.

INDEX OF AUTHORS

A
Arnold, Matthew, 80–82
Auden, W. H, 159–60

B
Brontë, Charlotte, 118
Brooke, Rupert, 6–8
Browning, Elizabeth Barrett, 30–32, 129–30, 167
Bryant, William Cullen, 122

C
Carroll, Lewis, 50–53
Chesterton, G. K., 12, 132, 140–41
Coleridge, Samuel Taylor, 20–21
Cowper, william, 207–08
Crashaw, Richard, 45, 133, 171, 199
Cummings, E. E., 115–16

D

Dickens, Charles, 1, 72, 75–77, 78, 79–80, 86–87,134, 146, 175–76, 212
Dickinson, Emily, 159, 169, 211
Donne, John, 53, 73–74, 161–62, 187–88, ·211–12

E

Eliot, T. S., 35–37, 47–49

F

Frost, Robert, 137

G

Goeth, J. W. von, 202–03
Graves, Robert, 60–61, 126

H

Hardy, Thomas, 194–96
Hawthorne, Nathaniel, 101
Herbert, George, 87–88, 90–91, 95–96, 142, 168
Herrick, Robert, 33, 113–14, 174, 193
Hopkins, Gerard Manley, 13–15, 84, 94, 197–98
Houseman, A. E., 112–13

J

Jonson, Ben, 24–25

K

Kilmer, Joyce, 18–19
Kipling, Rudyard, 119–21

L

Lamb, Charles, 102–04
Lawrence, D. H., 177–79
Longfellow, Henry Wadsworth, 37–40, 124,
135–36, 176–77
Lowell, Robert, 44–45, 122–23

M

Marvell, Andrew, 169–70
Merton, Thomas, 63–64
Millay, Edna St. Vincent, 71–72
Milton, John, 21–22, 33–34, 59, 152–53

P

Pascal, Blaise, 162–63
Pasternak, Boris, 28–30, 163–65
Pope, Alexander, 9

Q

Quarles, Francis, 91–92

R

Rilke, Rainer Marie, 10–11, 16, 157, 165–66
Rosetti, Christina Georgina, 22–24, 85, 88–89,
125, 128, 149, 154,
185–86, 189, 200
Rosetti, Dante Gabriel, 5–6, 106
Rostand, Edmond, 66–70

S

Sandburg, Carl, 25–27, 54

Sayers, Dorothy L., 97–100, 107–09

Schweitzer, Albert, 72–73

Shakespeare, William, 17

Sitwell, Edith, 180–82

Smart, Christopher, 92–93, 209–10

Spender, Stephen, 155–56

Spenser, Edward, 201–02

Stevenson, Robert Louis, 82–83

Stowe, Harriet Beecher, 190–92

Swift, Jonathan, 144–45

T

Tennyson, Alfred Lord, 131

Thomas, Dylan, 2–3, 158

Tolstoy, Leo, 56–57, 105, 143

Turgenev, Ivan, 116–17

U

Undset, Sigrid, 110–12

Updike, John, 203–05

V

Vaughan, Henry, 58–59, 62, 147–48, 150–51

W

Whittier, John Greenleaf, 183–84

Wilder, Thornton, 41–44

Wordsworth, William, 129